THE WORKING CULTURE:
BOOK 1
Cross-Cultural Communication for New Americans

David Hemphill, *Project Director*

Barbara Pfaffenberger, *Editor and Contributing Author*

Barbara Hockman, *Lead Author*

Denise Douglas, *Contributing Author*

Joanne Low, *Contributing Author*

Patricia Eisenberg, *Illustrator*

REGENTS/PRENTICE HALL
Englewood Cliffs, New Jersey 07632

Library of Congress Cataloging-in-Publication Data

Cross-cultural communication for new Americans / project director,
    David Hemphill; editor, Barbara Pfaffenberger;
    lead author, Barbara Hockman; contributing authors, Denise
Douglas, Joanne Low; illustrated by Patricia Eisenberg.
        p. cm.—(The Working culture; bk. 1)
    ISBN 0–13–965187–X
    1. English language—Textbooks for foreign speakers.   2. Readers—
Intercultural communication.   3. Readers—Vocational guidance.
4. Intercultural communication.   5. Vocational guidance.
I. Hemphill, David (date).   II. Pfaffenberger, Barbara
(date).   III. Hockman, Barbara   IV. Series.
    PE1128.W7594 bk. 1
    428.6′4 s—dc19
    [428.6′4]   88–15614
                            CIP

**Editorial/production supervision
and interior design:** F. Hubert
Cover design: Lundgren Graphics, Ltd.
Manufacturing buyer: Laura Crossland

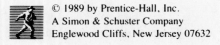 © 1989 by Prentice-Hall, Inc.
A Simon & Schuster Company
Englewood Cliffs, New Jersey 07632

Printed in the United States of America
10   9   8   7   6   5   4   3

ISBN   0-13-965187-X

Prentice-Hall International (UK) Limited, *London*
Prentice-Hall of Australia Pty., Limited, *Sydney*
Prentice-Hall Canada Inc., *Toronto*
Prentice-Hall Hispanoamericana, S.A., *Mexico*
Prentice-Hall of India Private Limited, *New Delhi*
Prentice-Hall of Japan, Inc., *Tokyo*
Simon & Schuster Asia Pte. Ltd., *Singapore*
Editora Prentice-Hall do Brasil, Ltda., *Rio de Janeiro*

Contents

To the Instructor

■ *NOTE*

The accompanying Teacher's Guide should be studied before the presentation of each lesson. This comprehensive guide provides complete lesson objectives and extensive culture notes with important background information and insights. The instructions for each activity give step-by-step guidance and specific factual information.

The activities in the student book are at a linguistic level accessible to the "low intermediate" student and are as self-explanatory as possible at that level. However, apparently simple activities are associated with more complex information and ideas, which are detailed in the Teacher's Guide.

Philosophy and Approach

The Working Culture: Cross-Cultural Communication for New Americans is one of a two-book set of activities for guiding newcomers in their job and career plans and for enhancing the cross-cultural understanding that is needed for these plans. Although English communication is certainly *developed*, the book is *not* designed as a *language-teaching text*.

The lessons are constructed around cultural and vocational concepts and apply these thoughts, ideas, and attitudes to varying situations. The aim is to spark awareness and open up discussion of important vocational and interpersonal issues as they are found in the United States in comparision with other countries. Individual students are expected to create their own responses, just as they will find and develop varying accommodations to their life situations. The lessons succeed when critical thinking has begun, not when issues have been neatly resolved. Right answers and neatly pat solutions are not expected for many of these open-ended activities.

Key Features

Cross-cultural comparison is emphasized. Training literature in cross-cultural communication consistently argues that the capacity for handling cultural transition is enhanced when one consciously reflects **both** on the **home culture** and the **new culture.**

Practical, immediately useful information about worklife, values, and social customs in the United States is the basis of the lessons.

The book is a "bank" of activities and not a developmentally sequenced course. The lessons can be sequenced to best meet the needs of the local program or classroom context.

Project Sponsor with major funding from the Ford Foundation

The Consortium on Employment Communication began in 1983 with major funding from the Ford Foundation. The Consortium's goal is to link linguistic minorities with the workplace. The Consortium's activities include developing instructional resources, impacting public policy, training staff, and conducting research.

Rita Cepeda
State Chancellor's Office
California Community Colleges
Sacramento, CA

Vy Trac Do
Fullerton College
Fullerton, CA

Carlos Gonzales
Adult, Alternative, and
Continuing Education
State Department of Education
Sacramento, CA

David Hemphill
San Francisco State University
San Francisco, CA

Autumn Keltner
Educational Consultant
San Diego, CA

Than Pok
United Cambodian Community
Long Beach, CA

Dale Rezabek
State Chancellor's Office
California Community Colleges
Sacramento, CA

K. Lynn Savage
Centers Division
San Francisco Community
College District
San Francisco, CA

Karen Thaxton
San Diego Regional
Employment Consortium
San Diego, CA

Chui Lim Tsang
Career Resources Development
Center
San Francisco, CA

Ford Foundation Representative: Patricia Biggers

Nick Kremer, Director
Consortium on Employment Communication
California State University, Long Beach

CHAPTER 1

Taking a Look at Cultures

In this chapter you will

- learn about the word *culture* and what it means.

- think about both your own culture and the culture in the United States and compare them.

- think about ways of keeping your own customs in the United States.

- learn about some American customs.

John Pitkin

LESSON 1: CULTURE IS . . .

Introduction

You came to a new country. Many things are different. Life in the United States and life in your home country are not the same. What is different? The customs and the culture are different.

Culture can mean a lot of things:

- how people eat
- how people think
- how people dress
- what kinds of families people have
- what language people use and how they talk together

What American customs do you like?

_____

What customs make you feel uncomfortable?

_____

What customs are hard to understand?

_____

Picture It

One difference between the United States and your home country is the **language.** Some words seem easy to translate. For example, think of these words in your language:

banana, water, man, tree, milk

What words are you thinking? Write them here.

_____, _____, _____,

_____, _____

Do you see pictures in your mind? What pictures do you see? Talk about the pictures you can imagine (see in your mind).

Here are some words in English. Write each word in your native language. For each word, draw a picture of what you see when you hear the word in your language.

| **In English** | **In My Language** | **To People in My Country** |
| *Words* | *Words* | *Pictures* |

fruit   _____

water to drink   _____

tree   _____

milk   _____

Now look at what people in the United States often see when they hear these words. Are your pictures the same or different?

| **In English** | **To Some People in the U.S.** |
| *Words* | *Pictures* |

fruit

water to drink

tree

In English

Words

To Some People in the U.S.

Pictures

milk

LESSON 2: WHAT'S IN YOUR MIND?

Now we will think about other kinds of words. These words tell about our daily lives, our feelings, and our beliefs.

dinner	a good husband	it's expensive
religion	a holiday	a good wife
the best job	transportation	sports
a house	a very good person	leaving home
a nice gift	a bad mistake	the future
a short distance	long hair	having a good time
borrowing money	a long trip	clothes

1. Read the words. Think about them in your country. What are you thinking? What pictures do you see in your mind?

2. Now work with a partner from your native country. The teacher will give you and your partner two words. Write down your thoughts and tell about the pictures you see. Write them in column 1.

The Words	1. To You in Your Country	2. To Americans in the U.S.

Now start over again. Read the words and try to guess what American people think. Your teacher will help you after you finish. Write your ideas in column 2.

■ *Discuss with your teacher and classmates*

Now talk with your teacher and classmates about the words and your thoughts about them (1) in your country and (2) to Americans in the United States.

LESSON 3: WHY AND WHY?

Are you feeling confused about life in the United States or about American people and American things? Do you wonder why the people here do some things? Do you have questions about American customs?

Write Down Ten Questions to Ask Some American People.

1.
2.
3.
4.
5.
6.
7.
8.
9.
10.

How to Get Your Answers

Your teacher will invite some American visitors to your class. You may ask the visitors your questions.

OR

Your teacher will give you a homework assignment. You will have to ask some American people by yourself, outside of the class. Your teacher will help you with the English.

LESSON 4: WHAT'S IN YOUR MIND AGAIN?

Here is the list of words from Lesson 2 again. You wrote down your thoughts and pictures about these words in your country. Then you wrote down what Americans think about the words. Now you will write about the same words again. Think about what the words mean **to you** in the United States. For example, *dinner*. What is it *to you* in the United States? Do you eat different foods here than you ate in your country? Is the time you eat different? Is the place you eat different?

dinner	a good husband	it's expensive
religion	a holiday	a good wife
the best job	transportation	sports
a house	a very good person	leaving home
a nice gift	a bad mistake	the future
a short distance	long hair	having a good time
borrowing money	a long trip	clothes

Write down your thoughts and the pictures in your mind.

The Words   3. To You in the U.S.

■ *Discuss with your teacher and classmates*

Now talk with your teacher and classmates. Compare list 1 from Lesson 2 and list 3 from this activity.

What pictures are the same? similar? different? very different?

LESSON 5: GIVING ADVICE

Everyone has problems. Sometimes you have a big problem, and sometimes you have small problems. Your small problem may be the same as another person's big problem. But all problems bother people and make them feel bad.

Now you have a chance to talk about your problems.

1. Your teacher will give you a small card.

2. On the card, you will write about a problem you have in the United States. Your problem may be small or it may be very big.

3. Your teacher will take all the cards and mix them up.

4. Your teacher will give you a card from another student. Read the other student's problem and try to find an answer. Sometimes it's easier to solve other peoples' problems than it is to solve your own!

LESSON 6: SIGHTS, SOUNDS, AND SMELLS

When we go to another country, we find a different language, different customs, ideas, and ways of doing things.

We also feel different things. For example, maybe you came from a country with hot, wet weather. Now you are in a place with cool, dry weather. So that feels different.

There are different sights for our eyes and different sounds for our ears. Also, there are different smells.

Think about how the United States feels. What is new or different to you?

What Looks Different in the U.S.?

1.

2.

3.

4.

5.

What Sounds Different in the U.S.?

1.

2.

3.

4.

5.

What Smells Different in the U.S.?

1.

2.

3.

4.

5.

CHAPTER 2

The Central Place of Work in American Life

In this chapter you will

- learn why work is a very important part of life in the United States.

- learn how Americans feel about work.

- talk about why people work.

Ken Karp

LESSON 1: WHO ARE YOU? WHAT DO YOU DO?

In the United States, people often talk about jobs or occupations when they meet for the first time. This means that jobs are an important way for people to tell one another who they are.

In your country, what do people talk about when they meet for the first time? What is important to them?

_____

_____

Here are some phrases that can tell who you are. Under the column **in my country** decide which ideas are more important than others. Write number 1, 2, or 3 next to each idea.

1 = very important

2 = sometimes important

3 = not very important

Who Am I?

In My Country		In the U.S.
_____	my village or neighborhood	_____
_____	my family	_____
_____	my job	_____
_____	my ethnic group	_____
_____	what I look like	_____
_____	my religion	_____
_____	the school I went to	_____
_____	my age	_____
_____	my political ideas	_____
_____	my hobbies and interests	

Do you think that the same things are important in the United States? Under the column **In the U.S.** write the numbers 1, 2, or 3. Discuss with your teacher and classmates what is different and what is the same.

■ *Discuss with your teacher and classmates*

When do people in the United States ask you, "What do you do?"

Why do they ask?

If you don't have a job, what can you say?

LESSON 2: IT'S JUST A SAYING

In general, American culture says that work is good. That means people *value work*. Here are some things Americans might say about work. Read each sentence. Draw a line from each item under **some people say** to an item under **they think**.

Some people say: because   **They think:**

■ Early to bed, early to rise, makes a man healthy, wealthy, and wise.

■ Take pride in your work.

■ God helps those who help themselves.

■ Work hard. Play hard.

■ The way you do your work is important. Work is not just a way to make money.

■ If you work hard, good things will happen to you. If you are poor, it's because you don't work hard enough.

■ It's good to work hard all day. Work brings good things to you.

■ It's good to be busy all the time—even when you are not working.

■ *Discuss with your teacher and classmates*

What do you think about these ideas? Do you agree or disagree?
Do you do any of these things? Which ones?

Ask some American people.

Do they agree with these sayings?
Do they do these things?
Do they think most Americans agree or disagree with these sayings?

In American culture hard work is valued. But many people don't really like their work. Even when people like their jobs, they sometimes complain about their work. Here are some negative expressions about work. (Sometimes people are only joking when they say these things.)

14

Draw lines between **things people say** and the **meanings**

Things people say

- Take this job and shove it.

- Now you've joined the rat race.

- All work and no play makes Jack a dull boy.

- It's time to go back to the grind-stone.

- TGIF (Thank God it's Friday)

- He's a workaholic.

Meanings

- It's not good to work *all* the time. People need to do other things.

- I really hate this job. I don't want to work at this job anymore.

- He works all the time. He never does anything else.

- You have to work, and commute, and do all the things other workers do.

- This was a hard week at work. I'm glad the weekend is here.

- Break is over. It's time to go back to this hard job.

■ *Discuss with your teacher and classmates*

Have you heard any of these expressions before? Which ones?

Do you have similar sayings in your country? Share them with your classmates.

Ask some Americans what they think each saying means. Share their answers with your classmates.

CHAPTER 3

Together and Separate: Living and Working in a Multicultural Country

In this chapter you will

- talk about the different kinds of people in the United States.

- talk about why people get together in groups.

- talk about the kinds of groups that people make.

- think about how to get along well with all kinds of people.

Ken Karp

LESSON 1: MANY KINDS OF PEOPLE

There are many different kinds of people in the United States and in this state. Are you surprised? CHECK ONE:
( ) not really   ( ) a little   ( ) a lot.

Did you know about American people before you came here?

Had you ever met any Americans?

Were you surprised when you got here?

You should understand the following words: **race, ethnic background, nationality, religion.**

What do they mean? Give an example for each word. Choose from the following list: Chinese from Vietnam, Caucasian (white), Buddhist, a citizen of Mexico. Your teacher will help you.

RACE _____

ETHNIC BACKGROUND _____

NATIONALITY _____

RELIGION _____

What Do You Think?

1. Are a Chinese American and black American the same **nationality?**

2. Are a Japanese American and an Italian-American the same **race?**

3. Are a Vietnamese American and a Mexican American the same **ethnic background?**

4. Are a Korean American and a Mexican American the same **religion?**

5. Are a Peruvian American and a Mexican American the same **ethnic background?**

You can make up more questions like these. Ask your classmates what they think.

1. _____?
2. _____?
3. _____?

■ *Discuss with your teacher and classmates*

Are you an American?

Can you be an American?

18

LESSON 2: ME, MYSELF, AND I

We are going to study about **groups.** But first, we will learn about **individuals.**

Game A: Who Am I?

Directions: Your teacher will ask you some questions. You will answer the questions and write a short story about yourself on a piece of paper or a card. *Don't* write your name or your country.

Your teacher will help you. Then your teacher will read the papers. You will guess who wrote each story.

Game B: I Like, You Like, We Like

The teacher will give you a card or a piece of paper. You will write some sentences about things you like and things you don't like. Then you will find out some ways that you and your classmates are the same or different.

LESSON 3: GETTING TOGETHER—MAKING GROUPS

In these activities, you will study about how people get together in groups.

Game A: The Tag Game, Stage 1

The teacher will tell you what to do. Then answer these questions.

Tag Game A: *Questions*

1. What did your tags mean?

_____

_____

2. What kinds of differences and similarities in people do they show?

_____

_____

_____

3. What were your groups?

_____

_____

_____

_____

These are differences we can see.

Game B: The Tag Game, Stage 2

Tag Game B: *Questions*

1. What did your tags mean?

   _____

   _____

2. What kinds of differences and similarities in people do they show?

   _____

   _____

   _____

3. What were your groups?

   _____

   _____

   _____

   _____

These are differences we **can't see** like people's ideas, beliefs, interests, likes, dislikes, jobs, and many more things.

People can make many different kinds of groups.

People can get together for different reasons.

LESSON 4: JOINING GROUPS

WHICH GROUPS DO YOU WANT TO JOIN?

I want to be with people who	Yes	No	It Doesn't Matter
speak my same language	_____	_____	_____
are my age	_____	_____	_____
are my height	_____	_____	_____
are my race	_____	_____	_____
watch the same TV programs as me	_____	_____	_____
are my nationality	_____	_____	_____
are in my class	_____	_____	_____
like the same sports as me	_____	_____	_____
have the same kind of family as me	_____	_____	_____
shop in the same stores as I do	_____	_____	_____
are my religion	_____	_____	_____
wear the same kinds of clothes as me	_____	_____	_____
wake up at the same time as me	_____	_____	_____
live on my street	_____	_____	_____
have the same ideas as me	_____	_____	_____

Discuss the list with your teacher and classmates.

Kinds of Groups in the United States

People form many different kinds of groups. Americans make groups for sports, for studying something, for taking trips, and others.

One kind of group is an **ethnic background** and **language group.** This is a group of people who have the same ethnic background and speak the same language.

Give some examples.

_____

_____

Who are these people? Are they *all* immigrants and refugees?

They may be "second-generation" or "third-generation" Americans. They get together and keep some of the culture and customs of the countries they or their ancestors came from. They may have:

1. ethnic restaurants
2. magazines and newspapers in their language
3. TV and radio programs in their language
4. private clubs
5. ethnic stores and businesses

■ *Discuss with your teacher and classmates*

Why do people want to get together with other people who have the same ethnic background and language?

Is this good or bad?

How do you feel about it?

Who Do You Want to Talk to?

Read the situations. Do you want someone who **speaks your language** and has the same **ethnic background?**

PUT A CHECK

Situation	*I want someone who is like me.*	*It doesn't matter. Any good person is O.K.*
1. Your car is broken. You need a mechanic.	_____	_____
2. You need a haircut.	_____	_____
3. You are sick. You need a doctor.	_____	_____
4. You are going to a store to buy food.	_____	_____
5. You are going to buy milk.	_____	_____
6. You want to find out about the classes at a school.	_____	_____
7. You have to cash a check in a bank.	_____	_____
8. You are applying for a job. You have an interview.	_____	_____

LESSON 5: GETTING TOGETHER AND GETTING ALONG TOGETHER

Prejudice and Stereotyping

We are going to study how we think about other people. Often we **look** at people and think about what kind of people they are.

A. Look at the pictures on this page. Do you know which people are

strong	sick	weak	healthy
hardworking	rich	lazy	poor
loyal	single	disloyal	married
funny	honest	serious	dishonest
happy	good in English	sad	bad in English

A.T.&T. Co. Phone Center

Danny Lyon/E.P.A.—
Documerica

Bob David

Laimute E. Druskis

WHO Photo by L. Almasi/K. Hemzo

Neil Goldstein

24

B. Now look at your classmates and teacher. What do you know about them? Do you know which people are

strong	sick	weak	healthy
hardworking	rich	lazy	poor
loyal	single	disloyal	married
funny	honest	serious	dishonest
happy	good in English	sad	bad in English

■ *Discuss with your teacher and classmates*

How do you know this?

Talk with your classmates. Were you right about the things you thought about them? Ask them some questions to find out. For example: "Are you sad? serious? poor?"

What if you are wrong? What problems can you or other people have if you think things that aren't true?

PREJUDICE

When we have an idea about a person just **because** he wears **certain clothes, looks** a certain way, or is a certain **race or ethnic background,** this is called **prejudice,** and we are **prejudiced.**

For example:

We think someone makes a lot of money **just because** he or she is wearing a business suit. Is this true?

   or:

We think **just because** someone has light blond hair, wears jeans, and is from Southern California, he or she goes to the beach every day. Is this true?

STEREOTYPES

When we have an idea about a *whole group* of people, then we have stereotyped ideas.

For example:

We think that all Americans love hamburgers.

Is this true?   ( ) yes   ( ) no

Do some people have stereotyped ideas about Americans? Make lists of ideas people have about Americans.

Good Things   **Bad Things**

Some people think   *Some people think*

Americans are rich.   Americans don't care about their parents.

_____   _____

_____   _____

_____   _____

_____   _____

_____   _____

_____   _____

Do you think American people have any stereotyped ideas about your ethnic group? Make a list of things people think about your ethnic group.

Good Things   **Bad Things**

_____   _____

_____   _____

_____   _____

■ *Discuss with your teacher and classmates*

GETTING ALONG TOGETHER

What is your **race?**

What is your **ethnic background?**

What is your **native language?**

What do you think? Can you have friends who are different from you?

Can people marry people who are different?

Why do people like to stay with other people like them?

Problems at Work

What do people do at a job?

Can you speak your own language at work with people from your country?

1. while you do your work?   yes (   )   no (   )

2. during lunchtime and breaks?   yes (   )   no (   )

READ THE STORIES AND ANSWER THE QUESTIONS.

Lunchtime

It is lunchtime at your job. The employees go to a special lunchroom. All the Latino people sit at one table. All the black people sit at one table. All the Filipino people sit at one table. You are from Laos. There is only one other worker from your country.

1. Where are you going to sit? _____

2. Is it true that people always sit with people of the same race, ethnic, and language background? _____

   Why do they do it? _____

   _____

3. Do they have to do it? _____

   Does anybody *make* them do it? _____

Other Kinds of Groups at Work

You don't always have to stay with people who are the same race, ethnic background, or speak the same language as you.

People can be the **same as you** *in other ways*. Go back to Game A in Lesson 3. You wrote about yourself. Now find other people in the class who are similar to you. How many different groups can you join? Write the names of some of them here.

_____

_____

_____

_____

_____

The Fight

Your workplace has many different kinds of people. There are white, black, and Asian Americans. Also, there are immigrants who are Chinese, Latino, Filipino, and Vietnamese. Sometimes the white and black Americans say bad things about the Vietnamese. Sometimes the Chinese and Filipino immigrants argue.

One day a Chinese and a Filipino began to argue. Then they began to fight. After a minute, other Chinese and Filipinos came to fight too. The Americans told them to stop. They told the other Chinese and Filipinos, "Don't go to help them. Don't join them. You should stop them."

But the Filipinos and Chinese workers said, "If we don't help and join them, then our people will think we don't care. We have to help our people."

Then the boss came in and was very angry. He made those workers who were fighting take off a week without pay. He said, "If you fight again, you will be fired."

1. Tell the story in your own words.

2. Who began to fight?

3. Why did the other workers join the fight?

4. Why did the Americans tell them to stop fighting?

5. What would you do in this situation?

LESSON 6: WHO'S WHO—THE BIG GROUPS AND THE SMALL GROUPS

In the United States there are many cultures and groups. There is a **majority** group and there are **minority** groups.

Majority means more than half.

Minority means less than half.

Majority *doesn't* mean better or worse or stronger or weaker.

The **Majority culture** is called the **mainstream.**

■ *Discuss the following ideas:*

If you want to be in the mainstream, what do you have to do?

your work

[ ] yes　　[ ] no　　You have to work for an American employer.

your language

[ ] yes　　[ ] no　　You have to speak English *all* the time—at work and at home.

[ ] yes　　[ ] no　　You have to speak English *some* of the time— usually at work and at school.

your family

[ ] yes　　[ ] no　　In your free time, you have to do the things Americans do. You must give up the customs of your native country.

[ ] yes　　[ ] no　　Only mother, father, sons, and daughters can live in the same house.

your house

[ ] yes　　[ ] no　　You must live in a neighborhood where many Americans live.

[ ] yes　　[ ] no　　You must have the same kind of furniture and decorations that Americans have in their houses.

your food

[ ] yes　　[ ] no　　You must eat American food most of the time.

your friends

[ ] yes　　[ ] no　　You must have a lot of American friends.

Who's in the Mainstream?

Hung

Hung works as a car mechanic in Chinatown. He doesn't speak English very well. He lives and shops in Chinatown. His kids are in school at an American university. His wife works in a sewing factory.

Guillermo

Guillermo works as a technician in a computer company downtown. At work, he uses his American name, Bill. He speaks and reads English, but he speaks Spanish at home. His wife is a housewife. Guillermo and his wife usually cook Mexican food at home, but sometimes they eat out at American restaurants. Their kids are in elementary school in a bilingual program.

Judy

Judy works in an architect's office as a secretary. She speaks Vietnamese at home. She has some American friends she meets on weekends. She teaches them how to cook and eat Vietnamese food, and they teach her some American cooking. She goes to adult school at night. She's single, but she doesn't go out on dates.

Is Hung in the mainstream?   [   ] yes   [   ] no

Why? _____

Is Guillermo in the mainstream?   [   ] yes   [   ] no

Why? _____

Is Judy in the mainstream?   [   ] yes   [   ] no

Why? _____

Are you in the mainstream?   [   ] yes   [   ] no

Why? _____

Do you want to be in the mainstream?   [   ] yes   [   ] no

Do you have to be in the mainstream?   [   ] yes   [   ] no

CHAPTER 4

Standards of Politeness and Appearance

In this chapter you will

- learn about American uses of language and behavior to show politeness.

- learn how to understand body language.

- learn about what Americans wear to work.

- learn about the importance of personal hygiene in the workplace.

Ken Karp

LESSON 1: WHAT IS A GESTURE?

In your home country, what gesture do you use to:

1. call the waiter.
2. say "come here."
3. ask someone to wait and not interrupt until you are off the phone.
4. show agreement with something your supervisor is saying.
5. show disagreement with something someone is saying.
6. show that you can't hear the speaker very well.
7. show that you don't know or understand something.

Make a gesture for one or two of these ideas. Does the gesture have the same meaning for your classmates? Do you think the American gesture is the same as the gesture in your country?

What Do These Mean to You?

Did you or your friends use any of these gestures in your home country? If yes, do you think they have the same meaning in the United States?

1.

2.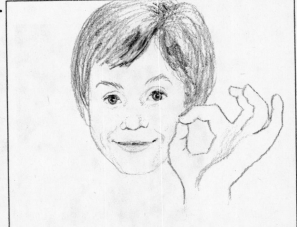

3.

4.

5.

6.

7.

8.

9.

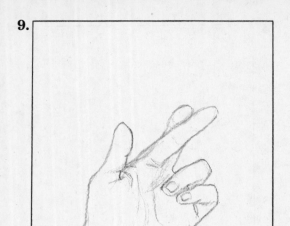

10.

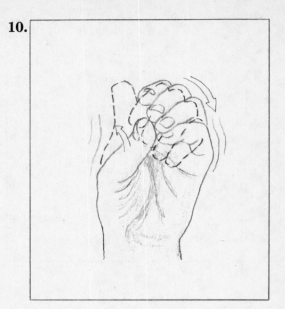

11.

What Does the Teacher's Gesture Mean?

Your teacher will make a gesture. Look at the meanings below.

1. I mean *you*.
2. I understand, I got it. OR I'm cool, I'm special.
3. O.K. Right. We did it. Everything is fine.
4. I'm angry at you.
5. I'm talking about money.
6. I'm hoping for good luck.
7. That person is crazy.
8. That's no good. Not O.K. We didn't do it.
9. I don't know. OR I don't care.
10. I mean *me*.
11. That person is very smart, intelligent.
12. I'm trying to be friendly with you. I want you to be O.K.
13. I'm proud of myself and I did an excellent job.
14. That's good. We did well.

LESSON 2: TALKING WITHOUT WORDS

Talking without words is **body language.** We can use our faces, our hands, and our body position and posture (how we stand or sit) to say things.

Facial expression means using our face. Make facial expressions for

happy   angry   sad   bored

Here are some facial expressions. What do they mean?

Eye Contact

The most important facial expression is **eye contact.** In the United States, people look at the faces and eyes of other people when they talk. This means they look at older and younger people, men, women, their parents, their children, their bosses, their teachers, and their friends.

What will most American people think if you don't do this?

Is it the same in your country?

In *your country,* who can each person look at when talking or listening? Put a check next to the ones the person can look at.

A Boy	**A Girl**
_____ his sister	_____ her brother
_____ his brother	_____ her sister
_____ his mother	_____ her mother
_____ his father	_____ her father
_____ his teacher	_____ her teacher
_____ his grandmother or grandfather	_____ her grandmother or grandfather
_____ his friends	_____ her friends
_____ someone older	_____ someone older
_____ someone younger	_____ someone younger

A Man	**A Woman**
_____ his wife	_____ her husband
_____ his children	_____ her children
_____ his parents	_____ her parents
_____ his grandparents	_____ her grandparents
_____ his boss	_____ her boss
_____ his teacher	_____ her teacher
_____ someone older	_____ someone older
_____ someone younger	_____ someone younger
_____ a woman	_____ a woman
_____ a man	_____ a man
_____ a friend	_____ a friend

■ *Discuss your answers with your teacher and classmates.*

Sitting and Standing

Sitting and standing are like talking without words, too. When you sit straight, it says that you are paying attention. When you lean, it says that you are tired. People get together in different ways, too. When a few people are talking together, how do they stand or sit?

Here are some pictures that show different ways that people stand and sit.

1. in a circle

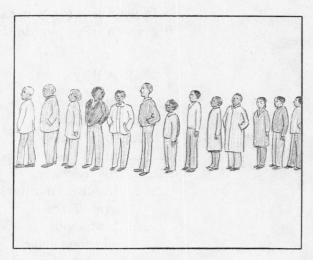

2. in a line

3. around a table

4. very close together

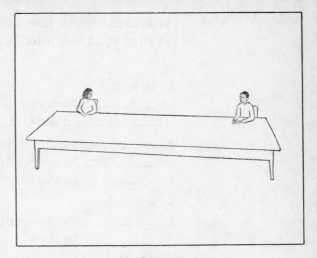

5. squatting   **6.** far apart

In a meeting at work, how do people stand or sit? Write yes or no for your country and the United States.

1. in a circle
   _____in my country
   _____in the U.S.

2. in a line
   _____in my country
   _____in the U.S.

3. around a table
   _____in my country
   _____in the U.S.

4. very close together
   _____in my country
   _____in the U.S.

5. squatting
   _____in my country
   _____in the U.S.

6. far apart
   _____in my country
   _____in the U.S.

At someone's house, how do people stand or sit? Write yes or no for your country and the United States.

1. in a circle
   _____in my country
   _____in the U.S.

2. in a line
   _____in my country
   _____in the U.S.

3. around a table
   _____in my country
   _____in the U.S.

4. very close together
   _____in my country
   _____in the U.S.

5. squatting
   _____in my country
   _____in the U.S.

6. far apart
   _____in my country
   _____in the U.S.

At a job interview, how do people stand or sit? Write yes or no for your country and the United States.

1. in a circle

   _____in my country

   _____in the U.S.

2. in a line

   _____in my country

   _____in the U.S.

3. around a table

   _____in my country

   _____in the U.S.

4. very close together

   _____in my country

   _____in the U.S.

5. squatting

   _____in my country

   _____in the U.S.

6. far apart

   _____in my country

   _____in the U.S.

LESSON 3: IS IT YOU?

Would You Do This?

Read the following list of behaviors. Do you think Americans show this kind of behavior? Would people in your home country show this kind of behavior? Circle yes or no.

	United States		Home Country	
1. You are introduced to a new co-worker. You shake hands.	yes	no	yes	no
2. You are waiting for a bus after work. The bus is crowded, so you push to get on.	yes	no	yes	no
3. You are in the company cafeteria. You are in a hurry, but you stand in line and wait your turn.	yes	no	yes	no
4. When you talk to your supervisor, you look at your supervisor's eyes.	yes	no	yes	no
5. You are introduced to your new supervisor. You bow to show respect.	yes	no	yes	no
6. You are walking toward the elevator after work. You say "Hi," to the new security guard. You don't know his name.	yes	no	yes	no
7. You want to get the mail clerk's attention. You snap your fingers.	yes	no	yes	no
8. You want to ask your supervisor a question. He is very busy. He is looking down at the papers on his desk. You walk in and interrupt him.	yes	no	yes	no
9. Your co-worker is giving his ideas on how to do a job. You keep quiet to show that you disagree.	yes	no	yes	no

What Would You Do?

Discuss the following situations. What would someone do in the United States? What would someone do in your home country?

1. You are 15 minutes late for class.

Home Country   **United States**

_____   _____

_____   _____

_____   _____

2. You are eating dinner at a friend's house. She is offering you more food. You don't want anymore.

Home Country   **United States**

_____   _____

_____   _____

_____   _____

3. You are walking down a busy street. A stranger smiles at you and says "Hi."

Home Country   **United States**

_____   _____

_____   _____

_____   _____

4. Your teacher gives you a homework assignment. You don't understand it.

Home Country   **United States**

_____   _____

_____   _____

_____   _____

5. Your co-workers are collecting money to buy a birthday gift for someone in the office. You don't know the person who will receive the gift.

Home Country   **United States**

_____   _____

_____   _____

_____   _____

LESSON 4:   MY LIFE IS AN OPEN BOOK

Sometimes we ask questions in a conversation to get to know the person we are talking to. There are some things that we think are all right for other people to know about. But there are also some things that we don't like to share with people we don't know well. Things that we don't want them to know are called personal things.

Look at the list below. Which things are personal in your home country? Which things are personal in the United States? Write "too personal" or "O.K." on each line

	U.S.	Home Country
marital status	_____	_____
age	_____	_____
salary	_____	_____
rent	_____	_____
cost of new car	_____	_____
number of children	_____	_____
personal problems	_____	_____
religion	_____	_____
job	_____	_____
love life	_____	_____
future plans	_____	_____
politics	_____	_____

■ Discuss with your teacher and classmates

Is the list for your home country the same as the one for the United States?

LESSON 5: WHAT SHOULD I WEAR?

Which of these people are probably at work? Why do you think so?

Hakim Raquib

Ken Karp

Marc Anderson

Eugene Gordon

Laimute E. Druskis

Laimute E. Druskis

Irene Springer

Laimute E. Druskis

What should a man wear to a job interview for each of the following jobs? Choose from the list of words at the right.

Dishwasher: _____

_____

Office clerk: _____

_____

Stock clerk: _____

_____

Janitor: _____

_____

Bank teller: _____

_____

shirt
tie
sport jacket
suit
slacks
sweater
blue jeans
sport shoes
sandals
regular shoes

What should a woman wear to an interview for each of the following jobs? Choose from the list of words at the right.

Kitchen helper: _____

_____

Bank teller: _____

_____

Office clerk: _____

_____

Hotel housekeeper: _____

_____

skirt
blouse
dress
jacket
party dress
suit
sweater
blue jeans
sport shoes
slacks
sandals
high-heeled shoes
flat shoes (leather)

■ CASE STUDIES

Directions: Help these people decide what to wear.

1. Jamie's friend works in an office. Most of the women in the office wear slacks (nice pants) and nice blouses to work. Jamie applied for an office clerk job at the company. Today she has a job interview. What should she wear?

    a. slacks and a nice blouse

    b. a nice skirt and blouse and a jacket

    c. her best party dress

    Why? _____

2. Bob and Sandra are new employees in the offices of Star Computer Products company. The employee manual says:

1. All men in the office must wear ties.

2. All women in the office must wear skirts or dresses.

Bob sees that some of the men wear ties, and some don't. Should Bob wear a tie? [ ] yes   [ ] no

Sandra notices that some days many of the women wear slacks to work. Some of them even wear blue jeans. Do you think there will be a problem if Sandra wears slacks to work? [ ] yes   [ ] no

Why? _____

Clean as a Whistle

It is important to wear appropriate clothes to work. It is also important to be *clean* and *neat*. Here are some things most Americans think you must do to be clean and neat. How often do you think most people do each one?

comb their hair: _____

take a bath or shower: _____

brush their teeth: _____

use deodorant: _____

wash their hands and face: _____

wash their clothes: _____

iron their clothes: _____

shave: _____

shampoo their hair: _____

cut their hair: _____

ACCEPTABLE OR UNACCEPTABLE?

ACCEPTABLE: When it is O.K. to do something we say it is acceptable. Example: It is acceptable to wear shorts at a picnic.

UNACCEPTABLE: When it is not O.K. to do something, we say it is unacceptable. Example: It is unacceptable to wear shorts to work in most offices.

Look at the following list. Are these things acceptable or unacceptable in your home country or in the United States? Write yes or no next to each choice. **Yes** means acceptable, and **no** means unacceptable.

chewing with your mouth open
———— in your country
———— in the United States

sneezing without covering your nose or mouth
———— in your country
———— in the United States

yawning loudly
———— in your country
———— in the United States

picking your teeth in class after lunch
———— in your country
———— in the United States

talking while chewing
_____ in your country
_____ in the United States

burping loudly
_____ in your country
_____ in the United States

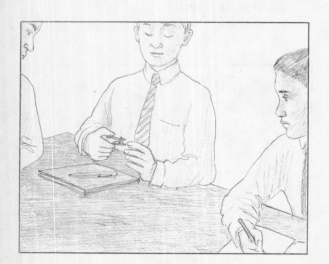

cutting your fingernails in a
meeting
_____ in your country
_____ in the United States

putting your feet on the table
while talking to a customer
_____ in your country
_____ in the United States

picking your nose in class
————in your country
————in the United States

Can you list other unacceptable habits?

1.

2.

3.

4.

5.

6.

Are unacceptable habits in the United States and your home country
the same or different?   same   different   (circle one)

■ *CASE STUDIES*

1. Phong is from China. There are students from many countries in his English class. Some students are from Mexico and Central America. Others are from the Philippines, and some are from Europe. One day after lunch, Phong burped loudly in class. Some of the students started laughing. Others looked very surprised.

   Why did some students laugh and some look surprised?

   If this happened in your country, what would most people in the class do?

   What should Phong do now?

2. Phong got a job in a small factory. His supervisor was American. One day there was a meeting of all the workers in Phong's department. While the supervisor was talking, Phong sneezed loudly.

   Phong's supervisor is an American. How do you think she felt when Phong sneezed?

   The other workers are from many different countries. How do you think they felt? Did they all feel the same?

CHAPTER 5

Implications
of Time

In this chapter you will

- learn what *being on time* means to most Americans.

- learn when and why it is important to be on time.

- learn how employers think about time.

Marc Anderson

LESSON 1: AM I ON TIME?

Directions: Read each situation. Think about your country first. Write the answer for your country. Then circle the possible answers for the United States. More than one answer may be correct.

1. A family invites you to dinner. They say, "Come at 7:00 P.M." You want to be polite. What time should you arrive?

   In your country: _____

   In the United States: a. 6:30   b. 7:00   c. 7:10   d. 8:00

2. You have a job interview. It is at 3:00 P.M. What time should you arrive?

   In your country: _____

   In the United States: a. 2:00   b. 2:45   c. 3:00   d. 3:10

3. You have a lunch date with a friend at a restaurant at 12:30 P.M. What time should you arrive?

   In your country: _____

   In the United States: a. 12:00   b. 12:30   c. 12:35   d. 1:00

4. You have a doctor's appointment at 10:00 A.M. What time should you arrive?

   In your country: _____

   In the United States: a. 9:45   b. 10:00   c. 10:05   d. 10:20

5. You found a new job. You are going to quit your job. When should you tell your boss?

   In your country: _____

   In the United States:

   a. at least two days before you quit

   b. at least two weeks before you quit

   c. at least a month before you quit

6. You have a job. Your starting time is 8:00 A.M. What time should you arrive?

   In your country: _____

   In the United States:

   a. between 7:45 and 8:00   c. between 7:00 and 7:30

   b. between 8:00 and 8:15   d. between 7:50 and 8:05

■ *Discuss with your teacher and classmates*

Are the rules about time different for work, home, and appointments?

In Your Country   **In the United States**

LESSON 2: TIME, TIME, TIME

Here are some sayings that show how some Americans look at time. Match them with the ideas they express. (Some of them are the same idea.)

A. Time is money.

B. A stitch in time saves nine.

C. There's no time like the present.

D. Better late than never.

E. Don't put off until tomorrow what you can do today.

F. Time waits for no one.

G. Time flies when you're having fun.

H. The early bird gets the worm.

_G_____ 1. Vacations and holidays end quickly.

_____ 2. Employers pay workers for the amount of time they work.

_____ 3. If you lose time, you can't get it back.

_____ 4. Do it now. Don't wait.

_____ 5. The first person to the sale will get the best bargains. The first person to apply for the job will have the best chance of getting the job.

_____ 6. It's not good to be late. But if you _are_ late, it's better to do something than not to do it.

What do _you_ think about each idea?

Tell your teacher and classmates about some sayings about time in your native country.

_____

_____

_____

Here are some short phrases about time. Have you heard them before? Do you know what they mean?

waste time   save time   kill time   lose time

In these examples, circle the phrase that tells what each person is doing with time.

1. It usually takes 15 minutes for Kim to get to work. Today the bus broke down, and she has to wait longer. She is

   wasting time   losing time

   saving time   killing time

2. Sara uses a copy machine at work. The machine is slow. Today she has to make a lot of copies. She is sending the work to a company that has a fast copy machine. She is

   wasting time   losing time

   saving time   killing time

3. Tai has a doctor's appointment. He gets there 15 minutes early. He reads a magazine while he is waiting. He is

   wasting time   losing time

   saving time   killing time

4. Esteban takes long breaks at work. He talks to his co-workers about things that are not important. He is

   wasting time   losing time

   saving time   killing time

YOUR LIFE

Tell your teacher and classmates about an experience when you

lost time

saved time

wasted time

killed time

Why are the following things important to Americans? What do they tell you about Americans' feelings about time?

instant coffee	T.V. dinners
fast food restaurants	1-hour photo service
automatic tellers	same-day cleaning service
overnight mail	while-u-wait shoe repair

Do you feel the same way about time? _____yes _____no

Why?

LESSON 3: HOW LONG DOES IT TAKE?

When you think of these ideas, think of the amount of time people usually take for each one. Is it the same in the United States and in your country?

For example: Is lunchtime 30 minutes? 1 hour? 2 hours?

	Your Country	U.S.
lunchtime	_____	_____
break time	_____	_____
a full workday	_____	_____
a work week	_____	_____
time to prepare dinner	_____	_____
dinnertime	_____	_____
time to get to work (travel time)	_____	_____
rest time or nap time	_____	_____

■ *Discuss the list above with your teacher and classmates.*

■ *Contact Assignment*

Ask other people from your country how long they take to do the things on the list above.

Ask some people from other countries how long they take to do these things.

Ask some Americans how long they take to do these things.

Name of Country: _____

	How Long?
lunchtime	_____
break time	_____
a full workday	_____
a work week	_____
time to prepare dinner	_____
dinnertime	_____
time to get to work (travel time)	_____
rest time or nap time	_____

Name of Country: _____

How Long?

lunchtime _____

break time _____

a full workday _____

a work week _____

time to prepare dinner _____

dinnertime _____

time to get to work
(travel time) _____

rest time or nap time _____

Name of Country: _____

How Long?

lunchtime _____

break time _____

a full workday _____

a work week _____

time to prepare dinner _____

dinnertime _____

time to get to work
(travel time) _____

rest time or nap time _____

LESSON 4: SORRY I'M LATE

Here are some reasons for being late to work. Are they good reasons?
Write yes or no next to each reason.

Your Country	The U.S.	
_____	_____	1. tired
_____	_____	2. appointment with social worker
_____	_____	3. met a friend on the way to work
_____	_____	4. dentist or doctor's appointment
_____	_____	5. errands (had to go to the post office, bank, or shopping)
_____	_____	6. family emergency
_____	_____	7. relatives visiting
_____	_____	8. bus was ten minutes late
_____	_____	9. bus broke down
_____	_____	10. sick

■ Discussion

Sometimes you have to be late. You can't help it. But sometimes you
can try not to be late. Look at the list above. What can you do to try not
to be late? Which things can't you change?

**Things you can do to try not
to be late:**

Things you can't change:

What should you do if you know you are going to be late to work? When should you tell the people in your workplace you are going to be late?

Write three good reasons for being late here.

Write what you should do about each reason here.
Your Country   *The U.S.*

With your classmates, think of ways to make sure you are on time every day.

_____   _____

_____   _____

_____   _____

_____   _____

■ *Discuss the list with your teacher and with your class-mates.*

LESSON 5: LATE AGAIN!

DANNY

Reading 1

Job

Kitchen helper in a coffee shop

Work schedule: 6:45 A.M. to 12:00 noon

Job duties: make coffee, prepare food for cook, wash dishes, put out cups, dishes, napkins, and silver for customers

Discussion: The coffee shop opens at 7:00 A.M. Danny is often a few minutes late. He gets to work at 6:55 or 7:00. Do you think this is a problem? Why or why not?

Reading 2

One day, Danny arrived at 7:00 A.M. The other employees were angry because they had to do some of Danny's work. The customers were angry because the coffee wasn't ready. The manager was also angry because the other employees and the customers were angry. Danny was surprised. He thought the other people shouldn't be angry. He was *only* 15 minutes late.

What do you think?

Circle the letter(s) of the ideas you agree with most. You may choose more than one idea.

a. Nobody should be upset. Fifteen minutes is not very late.

b. The manager is right to be angry. He might lose customers if the coffee is not ready.

c. Danny had a problem getting to work. The manager should understand this and shouldn't be angry.

d. It's all right to be late once in a while. But Danny is late often. So the manager has a right to be angry.

e. The other employees have a good reason to be angry. When Danny is late, their jobs are more difficult.

SAM

Reading 1

Sam works at a small hardware store. It opens at 8:30 A.M., but there are usually no customers until 9:00. The owner, Mr. Rigby, gets to work at 10:00. Sam works alone until Mr. Rigby gets there. Sam is almost always on time.

Sam has a young son. One day he had to take his son to the day-care center on his way to work. The day-care center opens at 8:30. Sam got to work at 8:50.

Discussion

Do you think there is a problem? Why?

What could happen?

Reading 2

That day a customer complained to Mr. Rigby. He came to the store at 8:30 to buy a hammer. But he had to buy the hammer at another store because Mr. Rigby's store was closed. Mr. Rigby talked to Sam about this. Sam explained his problem. Mr. Rigby was angry. He said, "How often do you do this? You should call me if you're going to be late."

What do you think?

Circle the letter(s) of the ideas you agree with most. You may choose more than one idea.

a. Mr. Rigby is not very nice. He shouldn't be angry. Sam was only late once.

b. Mr. Rigby is right. It is Sam's responsibility to get to work on time or to call him.

c. It is important for Sam to open the store at 8:30 *every* day.

d. It is not important for Sam to open the store at 8:30 *every* day. There are only a few customers at that time.

FLORENCIA

Reading 1

Florencia is a cashier in a toy store. She always leaves home early, and she usually gets to work 20 minutes early. Yesterday she left home 20 minutes early, but she was late for work because her car broke down. She was not near a telephone. She explained the problem to her supervisor, Mrs. Sanchez, and apologized.

Discussion

How did Florencia try not to be late?

Did Florencia do the right things?

What do you think Mrs. Sanchez will say?

Reading 2

Mrs. Sanchez was angry with Florencia. She said, "You should call and let me know when you are going to be late!"

What do you think?

Circle the letter(s) of the ideas you agree with most. You may choose more than one idea.

a. Mrs. Sanchez is right. Florencia should have called.

b. Mrs. Sanchez is unreasonable. Florencia couldn't call because she wasn't near a phone.

c. Florencia should explain in a polite way that she was not near a phone. She got to work sooner because she didn't spend time looking for a phone.

d. Florencia shouldn't explain anything. She should just say, "Yes. I'm very sorry."

e. Mrs. Sanchez is angry, so Florencia should be angry. She should say, "Look! I tried my best! That's all I can do!"

KHOA

Reading 1

Khoa is a good waiter. He worked at the Elegant Seafood Restaurant in Los Angeles for one year. His boss liked him. One day Khoa's brother came from San Francisco to visit. He asked Khoa to move to San Francisco. Khoa agreed.

When Khoa went to work that day, he said to his boss, Jake, "I can work today and tomorrow. Then I can't work here anymore because I'm moving to San Francisco."

What do you think?

Circle *one:*

a. There is no problem. Khoa has a good reason for leaving his job, and he told his boss he was leaving. Jake won't be angry.

b. Jake, Khoa's boss, will probably be angry with Khoa.

Reading 2

In San Francisco, Khoa applied for a job as a waiter. On the job application, he wrote Jake's name in the space that said, *References.* The manager of the restaurant called Jake. Jake said, "Khoa was an excellent waiter, but one day he quit. He only gave me two days' notice." The manager didn't give Khoa the job.

What do you think?

Circle the letter(s) of the ideas you agree with most. You may choose more than one idea.

a. Khoa was a good worker. Jake was wrong to say something bad about him.

b. The manager of the restaurant in San Francisco is stupid because he didn't hire Khoa. Khoa is a good waiter.

c. The manager of the restaurant in San Francisco is smart because he didn't hire Khoa. Khoa might quit this job without notice too.

CHAPTER 6

Work Is
Your Own Choice

In this chapter you will

- think about how people in your country choose their jobs.

- find out how Americans choose their jobs.

- think about how you can choose a job in the United States.

Celanese Corporation

LESSON 1: WHAT DO YOU WANT TO BE?

It is an American custom for adults to ask their children this question: "**What do you want to be when you grow up?**"

What does this question mean?

Why do people ask this question?

Here is a list of some ways that people choose jobs. Think about them, and fill in the chart. Write **yes** or **no** in each space.

Way to Choose Job	Is this done in the U.S.?	Is this done in your home country?	Do you like this way to choose a job?
1. Follow parents. *Example:* Patrick's father is a post office worker. Patrick will become a post office worker after he passes the post office test.	_____	_____	_____
2. Take over family business. *Example:* Sylvia's parents own a butcher shop. Sylvia and her brother Sam will run the business when they grow up.	_____	_____	_____
3. Told by parents what to study. *Example:* Teresa wanted to be a veterinarian, but her parents told her to be a nurse. She became a nurse.	_____	_____	_____
4. Told by a teacher what to study. *Example:* Jorge's teacher advised him to study engineering because he was good in math. He studied engineering.	_____	_____	_____

5. Told by a school coun-   _____   _____   _____
   selor what to do.
   Example: Barbara
   wanted to study busi-
   ness. In high school
   she took a special test.
   After the test, the coun-
   selor told her she
   should study for a
   "blue collar" job like a
   mechanic. Barbara de-
   cided to learn to repair
   business machines.

6. Told by a friend.   _____   _____   _____
   Example: A friend told
   Alvin to study electron-
   ics and get a job in elec-
   tronics. Alvin followed
   his friend's advice.

7. Do the work that is   _____   _____   _____
   available where you
   live.
   Example: In Dave's
   town, everyone works
   in the lumber indus-
   try. All jobs are part of
   that business. He will
   work in the lumber in-
   dustry too.

8. Other.   _____   _____   _____

■ *Discussion*

Now think about your jobs in the past.

How did you decide what job to learn or what job to take?

Did somebody tell you to take the job?

If you were still in your home country, how would you choose a job?

LESSON 2: DIFFERENCES OF OPINION

Sometimes people want to give us advice, but we don't agree with them. Their idea is different from our idea. Your **idea** is your **opinion.** Read these situations. Put a check by your opinion(s).

1. You are a girl. Your father is a dentist. His father was a dentist. You plan to go to school to become a dentist. Your mother advises you to become a secretary. You go to dental school.

   [   ] I think it's a good idea.   [   ] I think it's a bad idea.

   [   ] I might do this.   [   ] I wouldn't do this.

2. Your uncle is giving you money for school. He wants you to study business. You want to study psychology. He says, "If you take my money, you have to do what I say." You say, "Keep your money. I'll get a part-time job."

   [   ] I think it's a good idea.   [   ] I think it's a bad idea.

   [   ] I might do this.   [   ] I wouldn't do this.

3. Your father is a taxi driver. Your mother is a waitress. They want you to go to college and then get a job in an office. They say, "We want you to do better than we did." But you don't want to go to college. You want to go to a trade school and be an apprentice carpenter because you can make more money as a carpenter.

   [   ] I think it's a good idea.   [   ] I think it's a bad idea.

   [   ] I might do this.   [   ] I wouldn't do this.

4. Your parents have a farm. You have been working with them on the farm since you were very young. You worked after school and on your vacations. Now you've finished school and you want to leave the farm. You want to go to the city to find a good job and make money. Your parents are very upset by your plan because they want you to stay on the farm. You leave the farm.

   [   ] I think it's a good idea.   [   ] I think it's a bad idea.

   [   ] I might do this.   [   ] I wouldn't do this.

5. Your wife tells you to change jobs. She wants you to get a job with higher pay. You like your job, and you hope that you'll get a raise later. Your wife says, "I know people who work at your company. They have worked there a long time. They don't get raises." You quit. You find another job that pays more, but it makes you very tired. You stay at the higher-paying job.

   [   ] I think it's a good idea.   [   ] I think it's a bad idea.

   [   ] I might do this.   [   ] I wouldn't do this.

6. Your husband can't find a good job, but you can. Your job pays well, and it's very pleasant. You ask your husband to stay at home with the children while you work.

   [   ] I think it's a good idea.   [   ] I think it's a bad idea.

   [   ] I might do this.   [   ] I wouldn't do this.

LESSON 3: STUCK IN A RUT—CHOICE OR CHANCE?

Americans believe that they have freedom of choice and can decide for themselves which jobs to take. They believe that each person does only what he or she **wants** to do.

When people make decisions and do **only** what they want to do, we say they are **deciding freely.**

If a person has only one choice, or someone else makes the decision, we say the person is **not deciding freely.**

We choose jobs. Sometimes we choose the job we want. But sometimes we can't get the job we really want, so we take a different job. This means we have *some* **freedom of choice.**

Directions: Read what the following people say about their jobs. Do you think each one decided freely or not?

1—no, not freely   2—a little bit freely
3—almost freely   4—yes, freely

How Did You Choose Your Job?	Did This Person Decide Freely?
1. "Everybody in my town works for the electronics firms, so I do too."	no .... yes 1 2 3 4
2. "I'm not sure. I got the job, and I never had the energy to change. It's O.K. Not good, not bad."	no .... yes 1 2 3 4
3. "My cousin worked here and got me a job. The pay is really good, and I need the money. But the work is terrible."	no .... yes 1 2 3 4
4. "I had to leave and move to another city because the factory closed, and everyone got laid off. I took the first job I could get."	no .... yes 1 2 3 4
5. "I have to support my wife's parents and her sisters and brothers too, so I work at two jobs."	no .... yes 1 2 3 4
6. "I got this job because they have a strong affirmative action program (they hire a lot of minorities). The pay is good, but it's hard to get a promotion."	no .... yes 1 2 3 4
7. "The training program sent me to this job. The pay is too low, but I guess I should stay here."	no .... yes 1 2 3 4

69

8. "I was getting unemployment in-   no . . . . yes
   surance payments. My worker   1   2   3   4
   found this job for me. He said if I
   didn't take the job, my unemployment payments would stop."

9. "My job is far from my home. I   no . . . . yes
   have to commute one and a half   1   2   3   4
   hours each way. I like my job a lot,
   and there aren't any jobs where I
   live."

CHAPTER 7

What Employers Expect From Workers

In this chapter you will

- learn what American employers *want* and *don't want* their employees to do.

- learn what an evaluation is and how employees are evaluated.

- learn why evaluations are important and how they are used.

Marc Anderson

LESSON 1: WHAT ARE EMPLOYERS LOOKING FOR?

To *evaluate* means to tell how good or how bad something is. When employers evaluate employees, they say how well or how badly an employee does the job. Employers evaluate employees' job skills, but they also evaluate other things. In this exercise, write some things that "good" employees and "bad" employees do.

Good Employee

	My Country	*In the U.S.*
with the boss		
with customers		
with other workers		
in general		

Bad Employee

	My Country	*In the U.S.*
with the boss		
with customers		
with other workers		
in general		

LESSON 2: HOW DO EMPLOYERS EVALUATE EMPLOYEES?

Read the following information.

In the United States employers do job performance evaluations regularly. Sometimes they are every six months. Sometimes they are every year. Your supervisor usually does the evaluation. Supervisors evaluate:

skills (Can you do the work?)

accuracy (Do you make mistakes?)

responsibility (Do you do what you have to do?)

commitment (Do you believe the job is important?)

cooperation (Do you work well with others?)

amount of work (How much work do you do, and how fast do you do it?)

initiative (Do you offer your ideas, and do you do your work without being told?)

Evaluations show your strengths and your weaknesses. This helps you to do your job better. Supervisors also use evaluations to make decisions on promotions, firings, and raises.

Do employers do job evaluations in your country? How did you know that you did a good job? Make a list of ways to evaluate work in your home country. Your teacher will discuss each of these with you.

1. _____

2. _____

3. _____

4. _____

5. _____

LESSON 3: WHAT IS EVALUATED?

Your teacher will help you fill in the things to be evaluated.

Class Performance Evaluation Sheet

Name: _____

Use the following scale to rate your performance.

        5= Excellent   2= Poor
        4= Above average   1= Completely unacceptable
        3= Satisfactory

Rate your performance. Put a check in the column that describes your performance.

Areas for Evaluation:	1	2	3	4	5
1. _____	_____	_____	_____	_____	_____
2. _____	_____	_____	_____	_____	_____
3. _____	_____	_____	_____	_____	_____
4. _____	_____	_____	_____	_____	_____
5. _____	_____	_____	_____	_____	_____

Your teacher will help you fill in the areas for evaluation. Complete the evaluation sheets for the workers described below.

Work Performance Evaluation Sheet

Name: _____

Use the following scale to rate work performance.

        5= Excellent   2= Poor
        4= Above average   1= Completely unacceptable
        3= Satisfactory

Rate the worker's performance. Put a check in the column that describes his or her performance.

Areas for Evaluation:	1	2	3	4	5
1. _____	_____	_____	_____	_____	_____
2. _____	_____	_____	_____	_____	_____
3. _____	_____	_____	_____	_____	_____
4. _____	_____	_____	_____	_____	_____
5. _____	_____	_____	_____	_____	_____

EXAMPLES FOR WORK PERFORMANCE EVALUATIONS

Complete evaluation forms for the following workers. Use the forms below.

Janine O'Hare

Job Title: Senior Clerk Typist

Job Duties: Answers phones; types; trains and supervises six workers; organizes files.

Job Setting: A large corporation

Company Rules: Work hours: 8:00 A.M. to 4:30 P.M.
                              Breaks: 20 minutes each

Performance:

- types 70 wpm (words per minute) accurately
- friendly; likes to talk with co-workers
- takes 30-minute breaks
- almost always absent on Mondays; absent 6 days in the last 6 months
- attends night classes for training
- arrives about 8:10 A.M. 3 out of 5 working days
- always meets deadlines (always finishes work on time)

Work Performance Evaluation Sheet

Name: _____

Use the following scale to rate work performance.

> 5= Excellent   2= Poor
> 4= Above average   1= Completely unacceptable
> 3= Satisfactory

Rate the worker's performance. Put a check in the column that describes his or her performance.

Areas for Evaluation:	*1*	*2*	*3*	*4*	*5*
1. _____	_____	_____	_____	_____	_____
2. _____	_____	_____	_____	_____	_____
3. _____	_____	_____	_____	_____	_____
4. _____	_____	_____	_____	_____	_____
5. _____	_____	_____	_____	_____	_____

George Wabash

Job Title: Clerk Typist

Job Duties: Answers phones; types; trains and supervises six workers; maintains files.

Job Setting: A one-person office

Company Rules: Work hours: 8:00 A.M. to 4:30 P.M.

Breaks: 15 minutes each

Performance:

- types 75 wpm accurately
- likes meeting people
- usually takes 20-minute breaks
- always absent on Fridays
- arrives about 8:20 A.M. 2 out of 5 working days
- takes Saturday classes; wants to get his B.A. degree

Work Performance Evaluation Sheet

Name: _____

Use the following scale to rate work performance.

    5= Excellent   2= Poor
    4= Above average   1= Completely unacceptable
    3= Satisfactory

Rate the worker's performance. Put a check in the column that describes his or her performance.

Areas for Evaluation:	*1*	*2*	*3*	*4*	*5*
1. _____	____	____	____	____	____
2. _____	____	____	____	____	____
3. _____	____	____	____	____	____
4. _____	____	____	____	____	____
5. _____	____	____	____	____	____

Laura Morales

Job Title: File Clerk

Job Duties: Finds files for other workers; files papers, forms, and folders; types address labels.

Job Setting: A small clothing company

Company Rules: Work hours: 8:00 A.M. to 4:30 P.M.
　　　　　　　　　Breaks:　15 minutes each

Performance:

- types 40 wpm—makes some mistakes
- quiet; doesn't like to talk to other workers
- takes 15-minute breaks
- missed 2 days of work last year
- arrives at 7:55 A.M. most days; goes home at 4:30 P.M.
- usually finishes work on time

Work Performance Evaluation Sheet

Name: _____

Use the following scale to rate work performance.

　　　5 = Excellent　　　　2 = Poor
　　　4 = Above average　　1 = Completely unacceptable
　　　3 = Satisfactory

Rate the worker's performance. Put a check in the column that describes his or her performance.

Areas for Evaluation:	*1*	*2*	*3*	*4*	*5*
1. _____	___	___	___	___	___
2. _____	___	___	___	___	___
3. _____	___	___	___	___	___
4. _____	___	___	___	___	___
5. _____	___	___	___	___	___

LESSON 4: WHY ARE EVALUATIONS DONE?

Job performance evaluations are a big part of working in the United States. Are they important in your home country? Try to list all the reasons why employers do evaluations regularly.

1. _____

2. _____

3. _____

4. _____

5. _____

Employers keep these evaluations in a special file. This file is called your **personnel file.** What other things do you think employers keep in personnel files? Your teacher will help you. Write them here.

_____

_____

_____

_____

_____

78

LESSON 5: OOPS! I GOOFED.

What do you do if you make a mistake at work? Look at the possible things you can do. Write yes by the good ideas and no by the bad ideas for your country and for the United States.

	Your Country	U.S.
Admit that you made a mistake.	_____	_____
Say it was someone else's fault. (maybe the boss's fault or your co-worker's fault.)	_____	_____
Make an excuse like, "The sun was in my eyes."	_____	_____
Don't say anything and leave early before anyone notices.	_____	_____
Try to correct the mistake, but don't tell anyone about it.	_____	_____
Learn how to do the work right. You don't want to make the same mistake again.	_____	_____
Get angry with yourself.	_____	_____
Get angry with everyone around you.	_____	_____
Laugh about it.	_____	_____
Apologize. (Say, "I'm sorry.")	_____	_____

■ *Discuss your answers with your teacher and classmates.*

Everybody makes mistakes. It is easy to make mistakes when you are learning new things. Employers *expect* you to make mistakes sometimes. But if you make the same mistake many times, you might lose your job.

If you make a mistake, you need to decide what to do about it. Here are some mistakes you could make at work. Read them and decide what you should do if you are working in the United States.

Would you do something different in your own country?

1. Your boss asked you to mail a very important letter two days ago. You just found it in the pocket of your coat.

In the United States   **In Your Country**

2. You work in a film processing plant. A customer asked you to print two pictures. You printed the wrong ones. The paper used is very expensive.

In the United States   **In Your Country**

3. Someone called to talk to your boss. You took a message. When your boss called back, it was the wrong number. Maybe you wrote the number down wrong.

In the United States   **In Your Country**

■ *Discuss your answers with your teacher and classmates.*

CHAPTER 8

Social Relations on the Job

In this chapter you will

- learn how co-workers get along and what they expect from one another.

- learn about the kinds of friendships at a job.

- learn about getting along with your boss.

Jane Latta

LESSON 1: WHO IS MY CO-WORKER?

The **co-worker** is the person you work with. **Co** means together or with. Who did you work with in your country? Who were your co-workers?

Check yes or no:

	Yes	No
men and women together	_____	_____
people the same age	_____	_____
people who are older	_____	_____
people who are younger	_____	_____
friends	_____	_____
family	_____	_____
people who don't know each other	_____	_____

Now answer this question:

Who will *you* probably work with in the United States?

Check yes or no:

	Yes	No
men	_____	_____
women	_____	_____
people your own age	_____	_____
people older than you	_____	_____
people younger than you	_____	_____
your friends	_____	_____
your family	_____	_____
people you don't know at all	_____	_____

Tell your teacher and classmates the differences between co-workers in your country and the United States.

LESSON 2: WHO IS MY FRIEND?

Do you want to be friends with your co-workers? What kind of people can you be friends with?

Put a check beside all the things that you *want* your friends to be. No check means, "I don't care; it doesn't matter."

My friend

_____is a man.

_____is a woman.

_____is younger.

_____is older.

_____is the same age.

_____has the same kind of job.

_____has any kind of job.

_____has a higher-paying job.

_____has a lower-paying job.

_____is a new worker.

_____is an old worker.

_____is any person I work with.

Here is the same list again. Answer this question:

What kind of person can American people be friends with?

A person who

_____is a man.

_____is a woman.

_____is younger.

_____is older.

_____is the same age.

_____has the same kind of job.

_____has any kind of job.

_____has a higher-paying job.

_____has a lower-paying job.

_____is a new worker.

_____is an old worker.

_____is any person I work with.

■ *Discuss with your teacher and classmates*

1. "At a job in the United States, we can be friends with almost anyone we want. We can be friends with people who are older, younger, or the same age. We can be friends with people in all jobs. We can be friends with men and women."

   Do you think this is true?

   Do you like it?

   Is it the same or different in your home country?

2. "Often, co-workers in America—men and women—are as friendly as brothers and sisters."

   Do you think this is true?

   Do you like it?

   Is it the same or different in your home country?

83

LESSON 3: WHAT IS A FRIEND?

Here are some questions about **a friend.** Talk with your classmates about these questions.

1. Is there a difference between **a friend** and **a good friend?**

2. Do you have many friends? good friends?

3. What makes a person a *good* friend? What do you expect from your *good friends?*

4. How long does it take to become friends?

Casual Friends

Some friends are **casual friends.** The friends at work (our co-worker friends) are usually casual friends. This means that they don't continue the friendship outside of the job. They are only friends during the work time.

What Will Casual Friends Do? Put a check on the line that expresses your opinion.

	I think so	I don't think so
They'll eat lunch together.	_____	_____
They'll talk about their families.	_____	_____
They'll talk about things they bought, and how much they cost.	_____	_____
They'll help each other at work.	_____	_____
They'll lend money to each other.	_____	_____
They'll talk about their plans for getting another job.	_____	_____
They'll give advice and criticism.	_____	_____

What Do You Think? Put a check by the ideas you agree with.

_____ Casual friends are dishonest because they are only your friends at work.

_____ Casual friends are not dishonest. They really enjoy working with you, but after work you don't have a relationship anymore.

_____ A **casual friend** may become a **good friend.**

Casual friends at work are important because _____

_____

_____

LESSON 4: BEING A FRIENDLY CO-WORKER

It is really very important to get along with your co-workers—just as important as doing your work well. Here are some things people say at work to be friendly. Have you heard people say these things? What do they mean?

Directions: Read each phrase on the left side. Find the meaning on the right side. Draw a line between each phrase and its meaning.

- We're having a potluck lunch.

- Can you chip in for a birthday present?

- I'll take you to lunch.

- Morning. How's it going?

- Want to go to lunch with me?

- Let's get together sometime.

- Let's go out for coffee.

- Take a break together.

- How are you today? (A **greeting.**)

- Eat lunch together.

- I'll pay for your lunch.

- Let's meet and do something when we're not at work.

- Give a little money.

- Each person brings food. We eat together and share it.

■ *Discuss with your teacher and classmates*

What can you say if someone says these phrases to you?
Practice with a partner.

What Will They Think of Me?

Sometimes you may have special problems when you are trying to be friendly. Read about two people's special problems and try to help them.

Ed

Ed came from a Spanish-speaking country. The place where he works has a big lunchroom where all the workers eat. The Spanish-speaking co-workers always sit together and speak Spanish at lunchtime. Ed wants to improve his English, so he wants to sit with English-speaking co-workers. The English-speaking co-workers are friendly, and invite him to sit with them. But Ed still doesn't sit with them. He sits with his Spanish-speaking co-workers.

■ *Discuss with your group:*

Why do you think Ed doesn't sit with his English-speaking co-workers? What should Ed do?

Ahn

Ahn is the only Vietnamese person at her company. At lunchtime, the Filipinos all sit together and talk in their language, Tagalog. There are usually two other groups of co-workers. One is mostly all black people. The other is all white people, except for one black person. There are two Spanish-speaking co-workers. Sometimes, they sit with the black co-workers and sometimes they sit with the white co-workers. But usually they go out by themselves. Ahn doesn't sit with anybody. She sits alone.

■ *Discuss with your group:*

Why do Ahn's co-workers sit in groups?

Why does Ahn sit alone?

If Ahn sits alone and doesn't talk to anyone, what will the other workers think?

Do you think Ahn *likes* to sit alone?

If Ahn wants to sit with other people, what should she do?

LESSON 5: FRIENDLY PROBLEMS

Read this story.

Tran

Tran had a great friend at his new job. Rick was like a brother to him. Rick taught him a lot about the work. He was always there to help with problems. Rick and Tran ate lunch together almost every day. They talked about their families. Once in a while they went out to a movie after work, but they never met on weekends because they were busy with their families. The families met at the company picnic, and the children played together.

One day Rick said, "I'm moving to another city because my wife wants a divorce." Tran was very surprised and felt very sorry for Rick. Rick and Tran promised to write to each other. They planned to meet during a vacation or a holiday.

Tran got one letter from Rick. He wanted to call Rick but he couldn't find his telephone number. That was all. Tran didn't hear from Rick again and he was very, very sad. He said that he didn't want to be friends with an American again.

■ *Discuss with your teacher and classmates.*

What Happened?

Why didn't Rick write or call Tran?

Did Rick do something wrong?

Did Tran do something wrong?

Do you think Rick will ever write to Tran again?

How would you feel if you were Tran?

Read this story.

Lupe

Part 1

Lupe was very lucky to get a job, and she worked hard. Her supervisor, Elmer, always said good things about her work. He gave her more attention than the other workers. Sometimes they ate lunch together, and sometimes he drove her home from work. Lupe knew that Elmer was single, so she began to believe that he liked her in a special way. She began to fall in love with him.

One day when he was giving her a ride home, she started to talk about marriage and children. She was afraid, but she knew she had to talk to him about it.

■ *Discuss with your teacher and classmates*

What Happened?

What do you think Lupe said?

Do you think Lupe and Elmer understood each other?

Why do you think Elmer paid a lot of attention to Lupe?

What do you think Elmer said? Finish the story.

_____

_____

_____

Here is another possible ending to the story.

Lupe

Part 2

Elmer understood what Lupe meant. He smiled and told her that he was only trying to be a friend to her. He wanted to help her because she was very smart and because he liked the country she came from. Then Elmer told her that he was gay.

Lupe felt _____,
and she _____

_____.

■ *Discuss with your teacher and classmates*

What Happened?

What was the misunderstanding between Lupe and Elmer?

What should Lupe do now?

LESSON 6: YOU AND THE BOSS

There are no rules about how to be a boss. Some bosses are friendly and kind. They think about the employees' feelings. Other bosses are strict and businesslike.

Directions: Read each situation. Choose the answers you agree with *most*.

1. An employee works hard so the boss will like her.

   a. The boss should do special favors for the employee.

   b. The boss should give the employee an excellent evaluation.

2. Your boss comes to you and asks you for advice about some work. You think,

   a. This guy shouldn't be the boss. He doesn't know what he's doing.

   b. He's kind and smart to ask the worker's opinion.

3. A boss is very friendly. He calls the female workers "honey" or "sweetie."

   a. He doesn't respect his workers.

   b. He's helping everyone get along and feel like a big family.

4. An employee came in late and didn't explain or apologize. The boss is very angry.

   a. The boss should never get angry at her employees.

   b. The employee must explain and give a simple apology.

5. The boss is the owner's son. He's young and very strict. He won't let any employee disagree with anything he says.

   a. The employees should complain to the manager or to the owner.

   b. The boss has a right to do things his way.

6. A co-worker made a mistake. You knew it, but you didn't tell your co-worker when she was making the mistake. Now the boss is angry at you, not at the co-worker who made the mistake.

   a. The boss is all mixed up. It's his or her job to correct workers' mistakes, not yours.

   b. The boss is right. You should politely speak out when you see someone do something wrong.

7. You asked for time off from work to take care of a very sick family member. The boss said, "No. The work you are doing is very important, and you are the only person who can do it."

   a. This boss is so cruel and mean, you should quit.

   b. The boss understands you, but the work at the job is important and has to get done right away.

■ *Discuss your answers with your teacher and classmates.*

■ *ROLE PLAYS*

1. (For women)

    a. You are a waitress in a small restaurant. You accidentally drop some plates, and they break. The manager sees the accident and says, "Don't worry, sweetie. I'll get someone to clean it up."

    What would you say? How would you say it?

    _____

    _____.

    b. You are a waitress in a small restaurant. You accidentally drop some plates, and they break. The manager sees the accident and shouts, "Hey sweetie, you'd better clean that up fast before someone steps in it!"

    What would you say? How would you say it?

    _____

    _____

2. (For men)

    a. You are a waiter in a small restaurant. You accidentally drop some plates, and they break. The manager sees the accident and says, "You've got *butterfingers today, huh? Well don't worry about it. Accidents happen."

    What would you say? How would you say it?

    _____

    _____

    b. You are a waiter in a small restaurant. You accidentally drop some plates, and they break. The manager sees the accident and shouts, (says in a very loud voice) "Hey you! You'd better clean that up fast before someone steps in it!"

    What would you say? How would you say it?

    _____

    _____

3. A member of your family is very sick. Ask your boss for some time off from work so that you can take care of the person.

    What would you say?

    _____

    _____

*butterfingers: someone who frequently drops things.

CHAPTER 9

Problems in the Workplace

In this chapter you will

■ learn about common problems that workers have.

■ learn about common problems that employers have.

■ think about how you can solve some of these problems.

Irene Springer

LESSON 1: PROBLEMS OF WORKERS

What problems have you had *at work* in your country or in the United States? What *work problems* have you heard about? In the space below, make a list of these problems. Your classmates and your teacher can help.

1.

2.

3.

4.

5.

6.

7.

8.

■ *Discuss with your teacher and classmates*

Which problems happen in your country?

Which problems happen in the United States?

In the United States what can you do about each problem?

LESSON 2: NOW WHAT AM I GOING TO DO?

Read each case or listen to your teacher read it. Make sure you understand the situation. Your teacher will ask you some questions. Then choose the *best ending* for each story. Discuss your answers with your classmates.

1. Who Gets a Raise?

Esther and Linda are waitresses. They work at Joe's Café. They have worked about one year. They both make $3.35 an hour plus tips. One day Joe gives Linda a raise. She will now make $3.75 an hour. Esther is angry because her pay is still $3.35.

Choose the Best Ending

a. Esther is rude to Linda. She says bad things to her.

b. Esther asks Joe why she didn't get a raise.

c. Esther quits.

2. What Is Sexual Harassment?

Ansi does not like to work with Phil. Phil always tells her she is pretty. He asks her to go on dates. Ansi says no. Ansi just wants to do her work. She wants Phil to leave her alone. She feels uncomfortable when she works with Phil.

Choose the Best Ending

a. Ansi tells Phil why she is unhappy. She asks him to stop bothering her.

b. Ansi doesn't talk to Phil. She talks to her boss about the problem with Phil.

c. Ansi tells her boss, "I don't want to work with Phil. He's a bad worker."

3. Help! What Do I Do Now?

Felipe was an assembly worker. He was very good, so the boss made him a supervisor. He supervises four other workers. He is happy with his new job. He is important and he gets more money. But Felipe has one problem: Now he has to fill out forms. He doesn't know how to fill out the forms.

Choose the Best Ending

a. Felipe doesn't fill out the forms.

b. Felipe asks someone else to fill out the forms.

c. Felipe asks his boss or another person to show him how to fill out the forms.

4. Martha Gets Tired

Martha is an assistant in a print shop. Jeff and John are the managers. They both give Martha work. Some days she has too much work. Jeff and John are always in a hurry. They say, "Please do the work right now." Martha never has a break. She gets nervous. Very often, she has a stomachache or a headache.

Choose the Best Ending

a. Martha asks for a meeting with her bosses. She says, "I'm very nervous and tired because I never get a break."

b. Martha takes vitamins and works faster.

c. One day Martha throws the papers on the floor and says, "I quit!"

5. A Long Break

Tien is a gardener for a landscaping company. He works with a partner named Tom. Tom likes to talk a lot. Tien wants to be a good worker. He doesn't want to lose his job. He also wants to be friends with Tom. But he is afraid to talk to Tom all day because the boss might fire both of them.

Choose the Best Ending

a. Tien refuses to work with Tom.

b. Tien takes long breaks with Tom.

c. Tien tells Tom that he likes to talk to him at break but that they have to work more.

6. When Is the Lunch Hour?

Sandra is a clerk in a large office. Everyone takes turns answering the telephones at lunch. Sandra usually stays at work during lunch. She is taking English classes at night, and she does homework at lunchtime. Now everyone starts going out at the same time because Sandra is always there. They tell Sandra to answer the phones every day.

Choose the Best Ending

a. Sandra talks to her supervisor about the problem.

b. Sandra talks to the president of the company.

c. Sandra doesn't answer the phone because it is not her turn.

7. When Should You Quit?

Two years ago, Carlos got a job in a company that processes food. He started work with four others. They all ran machinery. The other four were promoted, but Carlos still runs machinery. He often asks his boss for a promotion. His boss keeps telling him, "Next week." When there are better jobs open, the boss hires someone else. Carlos is unhappy.

Choose the Best Ending

a. Carlos gets angry at the boss and yells at him.

b. Carlos looks for another job. He plans to give two week's notice.

c. Carlos decides that his work is not very good. He doesn't do anything.

8. Who Is in Charge?

Stephanie works in a television repair shop with Carlota, but she is not Carlota's boss. Stephanie thinks Carlota wears the wrong clothes to work. Carlota likes to wear a lot of jewelry and makeup. One day Carlota wears a party dress to work. Stephanie tells Carlota not to wear that dress to work again.

Choose the Best Ending

a. Carlota never wears the dress again because she is afraid she will lose her job.

b. Carlota listens to Stephanie. Maybe Stephanie is trying to help.

c. Carlota gets angry. She tells Stephanie, "You're not the boss. I can wear what I want to!"

LESSON 3: YOU HAVE A PROBLEM IF THE BOSS HAS A PROBLEM

Sometimes you are happy at work. You think everything is fine and there are no problems. But maybe your boss thinks there is a problem with you. In this activity you will have the chance to think the way the boss thinks.

■ ROLE PLAYS

The teacher will give you a situation to read. Imagine that you are the person in the situation.

Discuss the situation with your group. Then you will have a conversation with one person from the other group.

Role Play 1: The Silent Worker

The Boss (Stan)

Job: You are the supervisor of the shop in a factory.

Situation: You have a new worker named Liu. Liu works hard, but he doesn't speak much English. Liu listens when you explain things, but he doesn't ask questions, and he doesn't say anything. You are not sure if Liu understands. You want to know if he understands.

What is your problem?

Now go talk to Liu about this situation.

Role Play 1: The Silent Worker

The Employee (Liu)

Job: You are a factory worker.

Situation: You work hard. You like your boss, Stan. When your boss explains something, you always understand. So, you don't say anything. But your boss is unhappy. You want to know why your boss is unhappy.

What is your problem?

Why do you think your boss is unhappy?

Now your boss, Stan, is going to talk to you about this problem.

Role Play 2: Now What?

The Boss (Janey)

Job: You are an office manager.

Situation: You have a new typist named Kim. Today you gave her a list of names and addresses. You told her to send a card to each person on the list. Kim has to type each name and address on an envelope and put a card inside. Kim understood the instructions, and she didn't ask any questions.

When you came back from lunch, Kim wasn't finished with the envelopes. She found some addresses that she couldn't read, so she waited for you. You are angry because you have a lot of work to give Kim, but she has to finish the envelopes first.

When you talk to Kim, tell her what she should have done.

Role Play 2: Now What?

The Employee (Kim)

Job: You just got a new job. You are a typist in a big office.

Situation: Janey, the office manager, is your boss. Today she gave you some work to do. It was easy. Janey gave you a list of names and addresses. She said, "Send a card to each person on this list." You had to type an envelope for each person, and put a card inside the envelope. Janey left the office. Then you found some addresses you couldn't read. You stopped and waited for Janey to come back.

Now it is late. Janey just came back to the office. Talk to her about your problem.

Role Play 3: What Happened to You?

The Boss (Kevin)

Job: You are the manager of a large auto repair shop.

Situation: You have a mechanic named Jim. Yesterday he didn't come to work. When you called him, he wasn't at home. It was a bad day for you because you planned to give him a lot of work. You had to do the work yourself. Today is Jim's day off but he came to work to make up for the time he missed yesterday.

Now talk to Jim.

What are you going to tell him?

Role Play 3: What Happened to You?

The Employee (Jim)

Job: You are a mechanic in a large auto repair shop.

Situation: Yesterday you had a bad toothache, so you couldn't go to work. You went to the dentist. You tried to call your supervisor once. No one answered the phone. You waited a long time in the dentist's office. When you came home, it was late. You didn't call your supervisor.

Today is your day off. You are going to work because you didn't go to work yesterday. You think that today you can do the work you missed yesterday. When you get to work, you can tell your supervisor about yesterday.

What does your supervisor probably think about yesterday?

Now talk to your supervisor.

Role Play 4: I'll Do It My Way

The Boss (Francisco)

Job: You are the supervisor in a factory that makes car parts.

Situation: Your employee, Antonio, is a very good worker. He knows how to make many things. He is very careful. But he works very slowly. One day you talked to Antonio. You told him to work faster. But he *still* works slowly. You have to talk to him again about this problem.

Why does Antonio work slowly?

What will you do if he doesn't work faster?

Now talk to Antonio.

Role Play 4: I'll Do It My Way

The Employee (Antonio)

Job: You are a worker in a factory that makes car parts.

Situation: You are a good worker. You know how to make many things. You are very, very careful because you want to do good work. Your supervisor, Francisco, says you are too slow. He says your work is good, but you must work faster. You think it is better to work slowly and do good work. You can work faster, but you don't want to because you want to be careful.

Today Francisco, your boss, is going to talk to you about your work again.

What do you think he will say?

What will you say?

Role Play 5: Working All Day and All Night

The Experienced Worker (Alicia)

Job: You are a worker in a fast-food restaurant.

Situation: Everyone on your shift starts work at 7:00 A.M. Everyone takes a break at 9:15. At 11:00 everyone has lunch. There is another break in the afternoon.

There is a new worker named Sandra. She works very hard. Sandra never takes a break. She keeps working. At lunchtime, she sits by herself. She doesn't talk to anyone. You hear the other workers talking about Sandra. They think she is not friendly. They want her to take her breaks.

You think Sandra is nice, and you want to help her. One day you decide to talk to Sandra about this situation. What do you think you should tell her?

Role Play 5: Working All Day and All Night

The New Worker (Sandra)

Job: You are a worker in a fast-food restaurant.

Situation: You are the newest worker in the restaurant. You want to show the boss that you are a good worker.

Everyone starts work at 7:00 A.M. There are two breaks and a lunch hour on your shift. At break time, you are not tired. You keep working. This shows that you are a hard worker. At lunchtime you always sit by yourself because you are new, and you don't know any of the other workers. You think they are not friendly because they don't talk to you.

Do you have any problems at work?

What do the other workers think of you?

Now Alicia is going to talk to you.

CHAPTER 10

Expressing Emotions on the Job

In this chapter you will

- discuss how to show your emotions on the job.

- discuss how much of your personal life to share at work.

- learn a little bit about American humor.

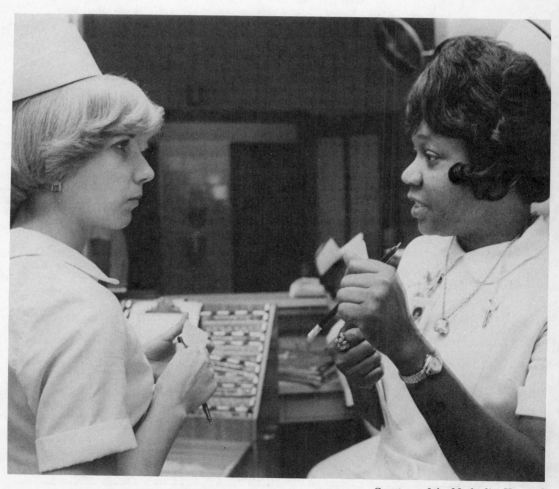

Courtesy of the Methodist Hospital

LESSON 1: WHAT HAPPENS TO MY FEELINGS AT WORK?

How Do You Feel?

All of us have feelings. Different things make us have different feelings. At work, what can make you feel

HAPPY?   FRIGHTENED?   EMBARRASSED?
ANGRY?   SAD?   DISAPPOINTED?
HURT?   PROUD?   NERVOUS?

Match the faces below with each feeling. Write the name of the feeling under each face.

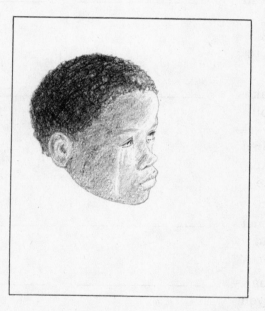

LESSON 2: HOW DO YOU FEEL? WHAT DO YOU DO?

Look at these situations. Write how you would feel if they happened to you. Then write what you would do.

	How Would You Feel?	What Would You Do?
1. Your paycheck is late.	_____	_____
2. It is almost time to go home. Your boss gives you a lot of work and says, "Do this now."	_____	_____
3. Another worker in the restaurant where you work says bad things to you.	_____	_____
4. A co-worker makes a mistake, so you and the other workers have to begin a job again. It takes 4 hours to do the job again.	_____	_____
5. Your work partner is being lazy and will not help you.	_____	_____
6. A co-worker laughs at you because you make a mistake. He says, "I made that mistake too."	_____	_____
7. There is money missing from your cash register. You don't know why. Your boss is upset and asks, "Why is the money missing?"	_____	_____

8. Your boss yells at you for a mistake you made.   _____   _____

9. You worked hard, but you didn't get a promotion. Another worker didn't work hard, but he got a promotion.   _____   _____

10. You always follow the company rules, but your co-worker doesn't.   _____   _____

LESSON 3: WHAT CAN I DO ABOUT IT?

Directions: Here are some short stories. Each story has many endings. With your teacher and classmates, discuss what will happen if the person in the story chooses each ending. Then write what you think is the best ending.

I'm Angry

Carmen is angry because she can't go home yet. She has to wait for Rosa to replace her and Rosa is late. Rosa is often late, and Carmen works overtime for no pay. What will happen if Carmen does each of the following things?

A. Carmen yells at Rosa.

Rosa thinks: _____

_____

B. Carmen leaves before Rosa arrives.

The boss thinks: _____

_____

Rosa thinks: _____

_____

C. Carmen yells at the supervisor. She says, "I'm tired of waiting for Rosa! Can't you make her get here on time?!"

The supervisor thinks: _____

_____

D. Carmen talks to the supervisor about the problem. She says, "I don't want this to happen again, and I want to be paid for the extra time that I worked."

The supervisor thinks: _____

_____

E. When Carmen has to replace Rosa, she will be late.

Rosa thinks: _____

_____

The supervisor thinks: _____

_____

F. Carmen does nothing.

Rosa thinks: _____

_____

The supervisor thinks: _____

_____

Carmen feels: _____

_____

What do you think Carmen should do?

_____

_____

_____

I'm Nervous

Sam has a job interview. He is nervous because he really wants the job, and he wants to do everything right. What will happen if Sam does each of the following things?

A. Sam says, "I'm not sure I can do this job. It sounds hard."

The interviewer thinks: _____

_____

B. Sam tells his friend that he is nervous.

After Sam tells his friend this, he feels: _____

_____

C. Sam taps his feet on the floor and chews gum.

The interviewer thinks: _____

_____

D. Sam says to the interviewer, "I'm a little nervous."

The interviewer thinks: _____

_____

What do you think Sam should do to help himself feel less nervous?

_____

_____

_____

I'm Hurt

Aurora works in a factory. She and her co-workers are working overtime because there is a deadline. That means the work must be finished at a certain time. Aurora is working hard and fast. Aurora and a co-worker stop for a few minutes. They need a short rest. The supervisor sees them and says, "All right, shut up and move it. We don't want to be here all night." Aurora feels hurt, and she thinks the supervisor is wrong. What will happen if Aurora does each of the following things?

A. Aurora throws down her apron and yells, "I quit."

The supervisor thinks: _____

_____

The other workers think: _____

_____

B. Aurora gets very angry and says, "We have been working very hard! You have to give us a break!"

The supervisor thinks: _____

_____

Aurora feels: _____

_____

C. Aurora says nothing, but she starts working again.

Aurora thinks: _____

_____

The supervisor thinks: _____

_____

D. Later Aurora says to the supervisor, "We were working, and I don't think it was necessary for you to yell at us."

The supervisor thinks: _____

_____

E. Aurora says, "I talk, but I work too. Look at this." (It's true that she and her co-worker did a lot of work.)

The supervisor thinks: _____

_____

What do you think Aurora should do? _____

_____

_____

LESSON 4: SHOULD I TALK ABOUT IT OR NOT?

Not everyone at work is your friend. Some people make decisions about how much money and responsibility you get. They also decide if you should keep your job or not. You have to see your boss and co-workers every day. If you decide you are sorry you said something to someone, you still have to work with that person every day.

Directions: Read the situations. Decide if you would talk about each one at work. Why or why not? There are no right or wrong answers to these questions. Discuss them with your classmates and your teacher.

1. You are dating one of the co-workers. You are very happy about it. Maybe this relationship will lead to marriage. But you are not sure about that yet. Do you tell anyone at work?

2. You are the only person from your country in your work group. It's a very important holiday for you. You have special celebrations and you eat special food. You are very happy and excited. Do you tell your co-workers about the holiday and explain it to them?

3. Some terrible things have happened in your country. You are worried about your friends and family that still live there. You are also very angry at the things that have happened. Do you talk about it at work?

4. One night you had a little too much to drink at a party. On the way home, you were stopped and arrested for drunken driving. Do you tell anyone at work?

LESSON 5: VERY FUNNY!

It's fun to laugh at work, but sometimes people's feelings get hurt. Read these situations, and decide what the person should do.

1. Sam's co-workers are teasing him. They are making fun of him. They say, "Look at this guy, he wears these funny shoes. He brings these strange things for lunch. He can't even pronounce the thing we are making and now he has an idea to make it better." What should Sam do?

   _____ Get angry and leave.

   _____ Laugh and repeat his idea for making the product better.

   _____ Say that he likes his lunch and repeat his idea for making the product better.

   _____ Start discussing life in the United States and life in his home country.

2. Susana had car problems this morning. She called to say she would be late. When she arrived at 10 A.M. her boss was sarcastic. He said, "Oh, good morning. Nice to see you here so early." What should Susana do?

   _____ Say good morning and get to work.

   _____ Say good morning and tell her boss about the car.

   _____ Say in an angry way, "I *told* you I was going to be late."

   _____ Laugh.

3. Kim is listening to her boss, Jim, explain something. An American co-worker is listening also. Jim is leaning back in his chair. Suddenly the chair overturns and Jim falls on the floor. He looks very silly. What should Kim do?

   _____ Ask Jim if he is hurt.

   _____ Laugh even though Jim looks unhappy.

   _____ Tell Jim to be more careful.

   _____ Ask Jim a question about the things he was explaining.

Remember: Some people are more *sensitive* than others. One person may feel very bad about a joke that someone else laughs at.

THINGS AMERICANS SAY

There are many American sayings about humor. Look at the list below. Read each one, and think about the stories you just read. What do you think each one means?

1. Can't you take a joke?

   a. You don't know how to tell a joke.

   b. Don't get angry. I was just trying to be friendly.

2. Laugh and the whole world laughs with you. Cry, and you cry alone.

   a. If you laugh at yourself you will have a lot of friends. If you get angry or sad, you won't have any friends.

   b. You should only laugh when someone tells a joke. You should only cry when you are alone.

3. Just laugh it off.

   a. Something bad happened, but don't worry about it.

   b. You should laugh at everything.

4. Laughter is the best medicine.

   a. You should only laugh when something good happens.

   b. When you feel bad about something you should try to laugh because it will make you feel better.

5. We're laughing with you, not at you.

   a. We want to make you feel stupid.

   b. We're laughing because we made the same mistake.

Write a saying about humor in your language, and tell your classmates what it means. _____
_____
_____

CHAPTER 11

Communication at Work

In this chapter you will

- learn how to understand English better, because you will know more about it.

- learn about different kinds of English and how to use them.

- learn how to understand and use English for informal and formal speaking.

Robert Houston

LESSON 1: DIFFERENT KINDS OF ENGLISH

1. Pronunciation Differences

People pronounce words differently around the United States. There are different *accents*.

A. There's a southern accent, a New York accent, a New England accent, a midwest accent, and others. Find out where these places are. Talk with your teacher about the different pronunciations.

United States of America

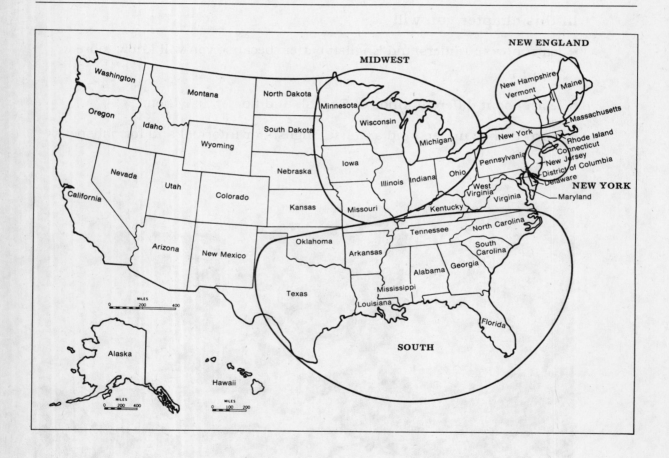

B. Are there different pronunciations in your country?

Which parts of your country have different accents?

_____ _____ _____

Draw a map of your country here, and show what parts of the country have different accents. Share the map with your teacher and classmates.

2. Dialect Differences

Sometimes people speak English in different ways. This depends on where they grew up and what kind of community they lived in. This is their custom or their style. It is another way of speaking English in the United States.

For Example:

Dialect	*Standard English*
A. What you doing here?	A. Why are you here?
B. I'ma help you.	B. I came to help you.
A. What for?	A. Why?
B. You busy.	B. You're busy.
A. Where your friend?	A. Where's your friend?
B. He been sick.	B. He has been sick.

You will hear many styles of English, and you will be able to get used to them and understand them.

3. Slang

English has a lot of special words for everyday conversation. We call these words **slang.** They change often. For example, one slang word is popular, but after a few years, people don't say it anymore.

Examples:

Cop is slang. It means police.

John is slang. It means a restroom.

Can you think of some English slang? Write it here.

_____

_____

_____

4. Idioms

English also has **idioms.** Find the correct meaning on the right side. (The idioms are underlined.)

1. Carlos: What do you think of the new boss?
    Lam: Just between you and me, <u>I can't stand her</u>.

    have a date

2. Cindy: How do you know Fritz is getting a raise?
    Edward: I heard it <u>through the grapevine</u>.

    not funny

3. Phil: Do you want <u>to chip in</u>?
    Sandra: What for?
    Phil: For Eva's going-away party.

    don't like someone

    a lot of people talking (gossip)

4. Karen: You know, Bernie doesn't want a better job.
    Helen: Oh well, <u>it takes all kinds</u>.

    give some money

    there are different kinds of people

5. Elvira: <u>How's it going</u>? Lemme see.
    Harold: Everything's O.K. I think.

    how are you?

6. Karen: Do you have a date tonight?
   Molly: Yeah. <u>I'm going out</u> with Pete.   a very good idea
   Karen: That jerk?
   Molley: He's not a jerk. He's very nice.   very serious
   Karen: If you want a date, you should put
          an ad in the newspaper.
   Molly: You're <u>as funny as a lead balloon.</u>

7. Bruce: I don't know what to do.
          This is a <u>heavy</u> problem.
   Sally: Come on, let's think about it.
          We'll get a <u>brainstorm</u>.

5. Jargon

English also has **jargon.** Jargon is words used by people in a certain kind of job or activity. Only people who work in that job use them. They tell about the work or the tools or something you do in the job.
Jargon is like slang, but it is for a special place.
What do these words mean to *you?*

mike: _____

lazy: _____

frozen: _____

bug: _____

Mike means microphone to people on television.

Mike means micrometer to car mechanics.

IOC means inter-office communication to office workers.

ICU means Intensive Care Unit to hospital workers.

Lazy means moving slowly to car mechanics.

Frozen means stuck, won't move to mechanics and technicians.

Bug means a problem to a computer worker.

Bug means a tape recorder to the police or a spy.

CRT means cathode-ray tube (T.V. screen) to people who work with computers.

What **jargon** do you know from a job in the United States?

_____

_____

_____

_____

6. Four-Letter Words

There are some English words called four-letter words or dirty words or curse words. Many people think that these words are bad to say. In the past, people didn't use these words. Now, we hear them more. People say them in the movies, too.

These words can be dangerous, so we don't want you to say them. But you may hear them, so we do want you to understand their real meanings.

Usually people say **four-letter words because:**

1. they are angry at someone or something.

2. they want to say something strongly—to emphasize something.

3. it is their habit or their style.

Examples:
Phrases That Often
Have Four-letter Words or
Other Curse Words   ***Real Meaning***

1. George: I can't find the _____   George is annoyed.
   outlet for this cord.

2. A: Hey, Sam doesn't want you to use   B doesn't care
      the phone.
   B: I don't give a _____
      I have to use it.

3. A: Why'd you leave your last job?   B feels angry about his
   B: Because of the boss.   last boss.
         That _____ expected me to
            work overtime with no pay.

4. A: I'm _____ _____.   A is angry.
   They're docking my pay because I
   was late.
   B: Well, don't be late.

5. A: Oh, _____! I forgot to go to   A is upset with himself or
      the bank.   herself.

6. A: Did you hear? We got a raise.   B is surprised and happy.
   B: Holy _____! That's great!

What Do You Think? You may check more than one of the ideas below.

_____ I think it's O.K. to use four-letter words.

_____ I think it's rude to use four-letter words.

_____ I feel O.K. if I hear someone else use four-letter words.

_____ I feel embarrassed if I hear someone use four-letter words.

_____ I feel angry if I hear someone else use four-letter words.

_____ It's all right if other people use four-letter words, but I don't want to use them.

■ *Discuss your answers with your teacher and classmates.*

7. Personal Styles and Cultural Background

There may be differences in English because of someone's **cultural background** and **personal style**.

Some people come from a home where the custom is **to stay very quiet** or to **speak softly**.

Some people come from a home where the custom is to **speak a lot** and **talk loudly**.

Some people always **complain** a lot.

Some people always **use four-letter words**.

Some people **talk very fast**.

■ *Discussion*

When you speak in your language, what is your **personal style? Tell about your style. How do you talk?**

When I speak in my language, I usually

_____ speak softly.

_____ speak loudly.

_____ speak a lot.

_____ speak a little.

_____ complain a lot.

_____ talk slowly.

_____ talk very fast.

_____ use four-letter words.

_____ use jargon.

_____ use slang.

_____ talk differently with different people.

_____ other: _____

When I speak in English, I usually

_____ speak softly.

_____ speak loudly.

_____ speak a lot.

_____ speak a little.

_____ complain a lot.

_____ talk slowly.

_____ talk very fast.

_____ use four-letter words.

_____ use jargon.

_____ use slang.

_____ talk differently with different people.

_____ other: _____

DIFFERENT WAYS OF TALKING

Read the different ways of talking. Compare people in the United States with people in your country. Put a check in the appropriate column.

Who?	People in the U.S.	People in My Country	It's the Same
Who talks louder?	_____	_____	_____
Who talks faster?	_____	_____	_____
Who talks more?	_____	_____	_____
Who talks more often?	_____	_____	_____
Who doesn't like silence?	_____	_____	_____
Who can talk in a hurry?	_____	_____	_____
Who uses shorter words?	_____	_____	_____
Who speaks in a higher voice?	_____	_____	_____

Where and When:	People in the U.S.	People in My Country	It's the Same
Who talks more while they eat?	_____	_____	_____
Who talks more while they work?	_____	_____	_____
Who talks more on the bus?	_____	_____	_____
Who talks more at the supermarket?	_____	_____	_____
Who talks more in the library?	_____	_____	_____
Who talks more in the movies?	_____	_____	_____

LESSON 2: DOING THINGS WITH WORDS—"How do you . . .?"

When we talk, our words **do** things for us. They are like tools. For example, I say, "**Would you pass me the salt, please?**"

What am I **doing?**

I am **requesting** (**asking for**) something from you.

People with **different customs** may **do** things with words **differently.** Here are some things we can do with words.

1. Ask for help.
2. Give advice or suggest something.
3. Make sure we understand.
4. Say we can't do something.
5. Say we don't understand.
6. Give someone a compliment.
7. Receive a compliment. (know what to say when someone says something nice)
8. Thank someone.
9. Say we don't like something.
10. Make a request.
11. Show we understand.
12. Apologize.
13. Criticize someone or something.
14. Give information.
15. Refuse a request. (say we can't do something or don't want to do something)

Here are some short conversations. What are the people doing?

1. A—Would you be able to stay overtime today?
B—Well I'm sorry, but I have something important to do after work today.

Person A is

_____ giving advice.

_____ making a request.

_____ making sure the other person understands.

Person B is

_____ refusing a request politely.

_____ making sure the other person understands.

_____ criticizing someone.

2. A—I told you to put the red ones over here, not there.
B—Yeah, I guess I forgot. I'm sorry.

Person A is

_____ asking for help.

_____ giving a compliment.

_____ criticizing someone.

Person B is

_____ asking for help.

_____ apologizing.

_____ saying he can't do something.

3. A—Would you help me with this?
B—Sorry, I haven't learned how to use that machine.

Person A is

_____ giving advice.

_____ criticizing someone.

_____ asking for help.

Person B is

_____ showing he doesn't understand.

_____ saying he can't do something.

_____ saying he doesn't like something.

4. A—Why don't you do the small ones first? That's easier.
B—That's a good idea. Thanks for telling me.

Person A is

_____ giving advice.

_____ criticizing someone or something.

_____ asking for help.

Person B is

_____ receiving a compliment.

_____ giving thanks.

_____ apologizing.

5. A—Hey, did you get a new watch? Wow, that's nice!
B—Oh, thank you. It wasn't very expensive.

Person A is

_____ asking for help.

_____ giving advice.

_____ giving a compliment.

Person B is

_____ giving thanks.

_____ receiving a compliment.

_____ giving information.

6. A—Look at this. You've done it all wrong.
B—What? I don't get what you mean.

Person A is

_____ saying she can't do something.

_____ giving advice.

_____ criticizing someone.

Person B is

_____ saying she doesn't understand something.

_____ making a request.

_____ saying she can't do something.

7. A—I'd like you to work the night shift this week.
   B—Well, I really prefer day or evening, if possible. I'd rather not.

Person A is

_____ criticizing someone.

_____ apologizing.

_____ making a request.

Person B is

_____ refusing a request.

_____ saying he doesn't like something.

_____ showing he understands.

8. A—So that's how you get to the stockroom from here . . . O.K.?
   B—Could you just tell me which floor it is again?

Person A is

_____ giving a compliment.

_____ giving information.

_____ making a request.

Person B is

_____ saying she doesn't understand.

_____ making sure she understands.

_____ making a request.

Now read the list of **things we do with words** again.

Can you do these things in English?

Check off **yes** or **no** on the right side of the list.

	Can You Do These Things in English? (Put a check)	
Here Is the List of Things We Can Do With Words From Page 122.	*Yes*	*No*
1. Ask for help.	_____	_____
2. Give advice/suggest something.	_____	_____
3. Make sure we understand	_____	_____
4. Say we can't do something.	_____	_____
5. Say we don't understand.	_____	_____
6. Give someone a compliment. (say something nice to someone.)	_____	_____
7. Receive a compliment. (know what to say when someone says something nice)	_____	_____
8. Thank someone.	_____	_____
9. Say we don't like something.	_____	_____
10. Make a request.	_____	_____
11. Show we understand.	_____	_____
12. Apologize.	_____	_____
13. Criticize someone or something.	_____	_____
14. Give information.	_____	_____
15. Refuse a request. (say we can't or don't want to do something)	_____	_____

LESSON 3: SPEAKING SUITABLY: WATCH YOUR MOUTH!

Read these examples:

Your co-worker answers a telephone and says to you,
1. "Excuse me, but I think there's a call for you on line 2."
2. "Randy, you have a call on line 2."
3. "Randy, line 2!"

Now, answer these questions:

Is the meaning the same for (1), (2), and (3)?

Which one is the most polite?

Which one seems in a hurry?

Which one is O.K. to say to a co-worker?

Which one is O.K. to say to a boss?

What Does Polite Mean?

Here are some different ways of asking someone to close a door at work.

1. "Get the door, Marge, would you?"
2. "Do you think you could close the door?"
3. "Would somebody close the stupid door?"
4. "Close the door, please."
5. "Close the darn door."
6. "Would you mind closing the door on your way out?"

Read each sentence aloud.

a. Is it formal or informal?
   How does the speaker feel?
   Write your answers here.

   1. _____
   2. _____
   3. _____
   4. _____
   5. _____
   6. _____

127

b. Who is the speaker talking to?

a co-worker?

a boss?

a boss to an employee?

someone else? (a security guard, a janitor, etc.)

1. _____   4. _____
2. _____   5. _____
3. _____   6. _____

Who do you speak to **more politely** in your country?

Who do you speak to **less politely** in your country?

Think about it and give honest answers. Circle a number for each person. The **most polite** is 5. The **least polite** is 1.

a friend	1 2 3 4 5	a store clerk	1 2 3 4 5
a co-worker	1 2 3 4 5	your wife or husband	1 2 3 4 5
a boss	1 2 3 4 5	a bus driver	1 2 3 4 5
a stranger on the street	1 2 3 4 5	your teacher	1 2 3 4 5
your mother or father	1 2 3 4 5	your child	1 2 3 4 5
a waiter	1 2 3 4 5	the doctor's secretary	1 2 3 4 5

■ *Discussion*

Talk with your teacher about your answers. Compare these with what American people usually do.

Do American people talk more politely with family and friends or with strangers?

What does polite mean?

What does informal mean?

Can you be informal and polite at the same time?

Note: American people usually speak informally with people they know well. They speak more politely (formally) with people they don't know well.

WHERE AND WHY

Sometimes you can change your way of speaking **for different reasons.** Look at the examples and tell how the talking is different.

A. You to Your Friend:

"Could you help me carry this box upstairs?"

Is this request long or short? Why?

What are you asking for?

What special words do you use?

B. You to Your Friend:

"My car is in the garage, and I have to pick up my sister at the airport. I was wondering if it would be O.K. for me to borrow your car for a couple of hours tonight, if you're not going to need it."

Is this request long or short? Why?

What are you asking for?

What special words do you use?

C. You to Your Friend:

"Why don't you pick me up on your way to work tomorrow? My car's in the garage."

Is this request long or short? Why?

What are you asking for?

What special words do you use?

D. You to Your Friend:

"I don't have time to go to the bank to cash my paycheck. Do you think it might be possible for me to borrow a couple of dollars until tomorrow? I'd really appreciate it."

Is this request long or short? Why?

What are you asking for?

What special words do you use?

TALKING WITH CO-WORKERS AND BOSSES

IS THERE A DIFFERENCE?

Is it different when you talk to your co-worker and when you talk to your boss?

Read the list below.

Who would you say these things to *in your country?*

Who would you say them to *in the United States?*

Would You	**Write Yes or No**	
1. USE THE PERSON'S FIRST NAME? *Example:* "Hi, Joe. How are you?"	_____	Your co-worker in your country
	_____	Your boss in your country
	_____	Your co-worker in the United States
	_____	Your boss in the United States
2. USE THE PERSON'S FIRST NAME TO ANOTHER PERSON? *Example:* "Did you know that Joe got married over the weekend?"	_____	Your co-worker in your country
	_____	Your boss in your country
	_____	Your co-worker in the United States
	_____	Your boss in the United States

3. SAY "NO" TO A REQUEST?
   Example:
   Other person: "Could you
   help me with this?"
   You: "Sorry, I have to go to
   lunch now."

   _____ Your co-worker in your country
   _____ Your boss in your country
   _____ Your co-worker in the United States
   _____ Your boss in the United States

4. CRITICIZE; TELL SOME-
   ONE HE OR SHE IS
   WRONG?
   Example:
   "That isn't right!"
   "You did it wrong!"
   "Look! You made a mistake
   here!"
   "That's not the way to do it!"

   _____ Your co-worker in your country
   _____ Your boss in your country
   _____ Your co-worker in the United States
   _____ Your boss in the United States

5. SPEAK ANGRILY ABOUT
   SOMETHING?
   example: "I'm really mad! I
   just got a darn ticket for not
   stopping at the stop sign, and
   I *did* stop."

   _____ Your co-worker in your country
   _____ Your boss in your country
   _____ Your co-worker in the United States
   _____ Your boss in the United States

6. COMPLAIN ABOUT SOME-
   THING?
   Example: "The payroll clerk
   never gets my overtime hours
   correct. What's wrong with
   him?"

   _____ Your co-worker in your country
   _____ Your boss in your country
   _____ Your co-worker in the United States
   _____ Your boss in the United States

■ *Discuss your answers with your teacher and classmates.*

WHAT AND HOW

Think about how you are going to talk at work. Let's work on some examples.

1. Say No to a Request.

Other person: "Could you lend me a pen?"
You: "No, I'm using it now."

Is this polite? Should you say it to a co-worker? to a boss?

Make it more polite: _____

_____

2. Criticize. Tell Someone He or She Is Wrong.

You: "That's wrong!"

Is this polite? Should you say it to a co-worker? to a boss?

Make it more polite: _____

_____

3. Ask for Something.

You: "Give me a better one."

Is this polite? Should you say it to a co-worker? to a boss?

Make it more polite: _____

_____

■ *ROLE PLAYS*

1. Ask a co-worker if you can borrow a pen.

   _____

   _____

   _____

2. Ask a co-worker if you can borrow $1.00 until tomorrow.

   _____

   _____

   _____

3. Ask your co-worker to work your shift one day next week.

   _____

   _____

   _____

4. Ask your supervisor if you can borrow a pen.

   _____

   _____

   _____

5. Ask your supervisor if you can leave work early today.

   _____

   _____

   _____

6. Ask your supervisor if you can take next Monday off.

   _____

   _____

   _____